JESUS NOW AND THEN

D0872505

JESUS NOW AND THEN

Richard A. Burridge & Graham Gould

WILLIAM B. EERDMANS PUBLISHING COMPANY
GRAND RAPIDS, MICHIGAN / CAMBRIDGE, U.K.

© 2004 Richard A. Burridge and Graham Gould
All rights reserved

Published jointly 2004
in the United Kingdom by
Society for Promoting Christian Knowledge
Holy Trinity Church
Marylebone Road
London NW1 4DU
www.spck.org.uk

and in the United States of America by
Wm. B. Eerdmans Publishing Co.
255 Jefferson Ave. S.E., Grand Rapids, Michigan 49503 /
P.O. Box 163, Cambridge CB3 9PU U.K.
www.eerdmans.com

Printed in the United States of America

09 08 07 06 05 04   7 6 5 4 3 2 1

Library of Congress Cataloging-in-Publication Data

Burridge, Richard A., 1955–
Jesus now and then / Richard A. Burridge and Graham Gould.
p.   cm.
Includes bibliographical references.
ISBN 0-8028-0977-4 (pbk.: alk. paper)
1. Jesus Christ — History of doctrines. 2. Jesus Christ — Person and offices.
I. Gould, Graham.   II. Title.

BT198.B855   2004
232 — dc22
2004040379

For all the students at King's College, London
who take the Associateship of King's College (AKC)

Contents

PART II: THE EARLY CHURCH

Contents

Prologue

It was not yet noon but the Chapel of King's College, London, was already packed with hundreds of undergraduates from all disciplines — scientists, lawyers, dentists and medics, linguists, philosophers, students of the humanities and social scientists — squashed into the pews with others sitting on kneelers in the aisles. The audio-visual technicians were checking the camera angles and setting up the simultaneous TV relay to the big screen in the Great Hall below where those who could not get into Chapel were now starting to overflow. As we adjusted our radio tie-clip microphones and checked that the CD player was set up properly, my mind drifted back in time. What would the founders of King's College over 170 years ago have made of all this, I wondered?

The crowds of students in jeans and sweatshirts drawn from a wide range of ages, races, colours, faiths, and cultures were gathering for the first lecture of the Associateship of King's College of a new academic year. Yet the AKC was the first qualification awarded in 1835 by the College, which had been founded a few years previously by King George IV after a number of people including the Duke of Wellington, victor of Waterloo, but then Prime Minister, and the Archbishop of Canterbury had campaigned for a College in the tradition of the Church of England to counter-balance University College London, newly founded with no religious tradition or requirement. Therefore, the course had lectures in divinity and theology at its heart in order to help students relate their other academic studies to the Christian faith and to the world around them. If they passed the examinations and had satisfactory reports from their teachers and had attended Chapel regularly, they could be elected as Associates of King's College. Nearly a century later, when the University of London was incorporated, the religious tests for King's may have been abolished — but the AKC tradition continued. Across the world, graduates of the College are proud to display the letters AKC after their name, following their actual degree letters, to show that they undertook these extra courses. Today King's College is a vast enterprise with some 18,000 students and 4,000 staff arranged on several sites either side of the River Thames in central London: in addition to those in the Chapel or the overflow, many other students watch video recordings on our other sites later in the week. Yet the intention of enabling them to reflect upon the core ideas of the Christian faith and theology, biblical studies and doctrine, ethics and moral philosophy, religious experience and other faiths alongside their degree studies is still the same now as it was then as we try to relate the original vision of the founders of King's College to today.

Furthermore, even the topic had a similar intention: Jesus, now and then. As we enter upon the third millennium, what is the relevance of the person whose birth is the starting point of the first millennium? Yet Jesus continues to fascinate people as much in the twenty-first century as he has in the previous 2,000 years. In these nine lectures in the autumn term of a new academic year, we were going to try to investigate why Jesus still has such an effect **now**, today, and look back at his life and death and his impact on people **then**, and in the first centuries of the Christian Church — and to see if all those old debates had any relevance for us today. Two of us would share the teaching: the Revd Dr Richard Burridge, Dean of King's College, is a New Testament scholar who specializes in Jesus and the Gospels, while Dr Graham Gould, a Lecturer in the Department of Theology and Religious Studies, is an expert in early Christian doctrines and worship.

A little while later, Ruth McCurry, an editor from SPCK in London, came looking for a book to commission about Jesus and was amazed to discover so many students coming to listen to the AKC in the Chapel. And so the idea was conceived of a book based on the course about Jesus — now and then — to make this available to a wider audience outside King's College. Since we could only get down to writing 'now and then', we had to find an editor who could take the tapes of the lectures and start turning them into the basis of this book. Jane Collins, herself a writer, editor, and publisher over many years, offered to undertake this task and sat down to watch the videos and listen to the tapes. We are very grateful to her for her vision for the book and for the hard work in producing the first draft for us to edit and rewrite. We also want to thank Ruth and her colleagues in SPCK for their editorial work, and Eerdmans, our American publisher, for their design and production.

As with the original lectures, this book is a joint effort. Richard Burridge is responsible for Part I on the New Testament and Graham Gould for Part II on the Early Church; we shared the first chapter with Richard doing the first and third sections on Jesus today and early ideas about him, while Graham produced the second and fourth sections on the Christian tradition and its interpretations.

Finally, we must pay tribute to the students whose enthusiasm and interest make teaching the AKC such a privilege. As they themselves were a mix of all faiths and beliefs, so we hope that this book will attract readers from both within and outside the churches — anyone who wonders why Jesus was important enough to set the calendar from his birth **then**, long ago in the past, and what he might have to say to us still **now**, today.

The Revd Dr Richard A. Burridge
Dr Graham Gould

Jesus Now and Then

Jesus Now: The Start of the Third Millennium

As the new millennium approached, with all the celebrations planned and several catastrophes predicted, it really felt that something momentous was about to happen. With that one tick of the clock one era would come to an end and another come to birth. There was a great sense of expectation, which is difficult to remember with all that has happened in our personal lives and the political life of the world since then. In that atmosphere, many people thought about what they were celebrating, perhaps for the first time. Why the year 2000?

It was 2,000 years since the birth of a man who, more than any other, could really have been said to have divided history in two. What do we know about the man called Jesus of Nazareth? Surprisingly little. What we do know is not very promising. He never went to school, and may not have been able to read or write, although he could well have learned how to read the scrolls of the Jewish Law. Certainly we have nothing surviving written by him, nor do we have any indication that he ever wrote anything.

We do not even know when he was born or when he died. Notionally of course Jesus was born in the year 0, but this was based on the calculations in AD 533 of Dionysius Exiguus — which is Latin for Dennis the Short — and it turns out he got it wrong. Jesus was actually born a little earlier: maybe 4, maybe 6 BC. He lived a short life mostly of obscurity, in poverty, working as an artisan, perhaps a carpenter or a workman, in the north of a Roman province on the edge of the Roman empire. He had a brief public existence, but we don't know when it was or how long it lasted. The account in Mark's Gospel seems to record various events which could be fitted into a couple of months: John's Gospel makes it stretch over two or three years.

However long this period was, Jesus spent it wandering around, preaching and teaching in this outlying province of the Roman empire, and never went more than a couple of hundred miles from where he was born. He gained local popularity as a teacher, preacher and healer before falling foul of the authorities, being arrested and executed.

This is not an impressive record at first glance. It is therefore all the more extraordinary that the calendar we use is centred on him. Some people don't use BC (Before Christ) and AD (Anno Domini) any more, but BCE — 'Before the Christian Era' or 'Before the Common Era', as some people prefer. However we refer to this, the dates are still calculated by reference to him. Despite the little we know about him, and whatever your beliefs about him, the effect Jesus had upon people around him and upon millions since means that we cannot understand much about our history and our culture without understanding something about Jesus of Nazareth.

Whose Millennium Was It Anyway?

Our culture is fascinated by Jesus. When the Millennium Dome at Greenwich in London was being first suggested, the concept was to look at where we were in the year 2000 — Body, Mind and Spirit. Of course, as soon as 'Spirit' was mentioned, people were asking, 'Well, what about whose birthday it is? Isn't it really rather odd that he shouldn't be involved in some way? Shouldn't he be invited to the party?' That led to a great debate about the Spirit Zone, which then became known as the Faith Zone — a place to understand something of who Jesus of Nazareth was, the impact he and his followers have had upon the world in the last two thousand years and the role of all faiths in multi-cultural society at the turn of the Third Millennium.

I was brought in to do quite a lot of writing about Jesus for the Dome, including the opening statements for the Faith Zone and the in-

---

A Millennium Birthday Party

It's many years since the birth of the baby Jesus, yet he continues to have a huge impact. Christians believe he is the Son of God; Muslims revere him as a prophet, while others — including Sikhs and Hindus — respect him as a religious teacher. Many of no religious belief are inspired by his human example of teaching, healing and liberating. Two thousand years later, this 'birthday party' invites us all, whatever our beliefs, to look back at the period since that birth — and forward to the challenge of the new millennium.

(From the official brochure to the
Millennium Experience [the Dome], page 7)

---

troduction to the accompanying official souvenir brochure, just after the introduction by the Queen. Six million people visited the Dome. For the Faith Zone we shot eight films with the BBC about the impact of Jesus and his followers upon every area of British life — obviously worship, but also education, healing, the health service, justice, liberation, life and society. I was also involved with a huge exhibition in the National Gallery in Trafalgar Square in London called 'Seeing Salvation', which assessed the impact of the life, death and resurrection of Jesus on Western art over two millennia. Again, vast crowds came to enjoy it. You couldn't get away from Jesus in the year 2000, and the ripples from his life and teaching continue to spread today.

Jesus Christ Superstar

What if you go out for the evening? Both London and Broadway have had revivals of *Jesus Christ Superstar,* Tim Rice and Andrew Lloyd Webber's rock opera. This has Judas Iscariot as its main character, complaining that Jesus' followers have 'too much heaven on their minds'. The musical contains very little of Jesus' teaching, but follows the last week of his life, using particularly John's Gospel. After Judas has be-

3

trayed Jesus, he sings the showstopper song, "Jesus Christ Superstar," in which he says that he does not understand who Jesus is or what is going on; he wonders whether Jesus himself knows who he is and what he has sacrificed.

In many ways, Judas echoes the voice of Tim Rice, the writer, but also of many people who ask the question, 'Who is this person?' Elsewhere in the opera Mary Magdalene sings a beautiful love song, "I Don't Know How to Love Him," in which she says that Jesus is just a man, but in a way that suggests she's beginning to think that maybe he's *not* just a man. The album sold in enormous quantities, it grew and developed into stage shows in London and New York, a film, and recent stage revivals.

In *Godspell*, Jesus became a clown: again this was a stage show and film, and it reflected the period of the late 1960s and early 1970s — Jesus with the flower children and the Hippie culture. This included a treatment of many parables taken from Matthew's Gospel, and a great deal of fun and play. It is interesting to note that both shows ended with Jesus' death and portrayed no resurrection. *Superstar* ends with peaceful music to the theme of Jesus' burial, and *Godspell* ends with his corpse being carried across the stage.

Jesus Goes to Hollywood

Hollywood has a fascination with the person of Jesus: he seems to be big news at the box office. In 1927 Cecil B. de Mille's silent movie classic *King of Kings* was an extravagant and very reverent portrayal of Jesus on film. By 1959 de Mille claimed that over 800 million people had seen that film, and that he had introduced more people to Jesus through the film than anything except the Bible. During the 1950s and 1960s there was a rash of Hollywood blockbusters from *Ben Hur*, the 15 million dollar epic with Charlton Heston, to *Quo Vadis, The Robe, Barabbas* — all trying to reconstruct the time of Jesus and show people meeting him. In 1966 Pier Paolo Pasolini, an avowed atheist and Marxist, produced a black and white film, *The Gospel according to Matthew*, which he dedicated to Pope John XXIII, and which, strikingly, was a faithful reinterpretation of the text of that one Gospel.

In 1977, Franco Zeffirelli's *Jesus of Nazareth* was a TV blockbuster six hours long, mixing all the Gospels up but maintaining a very reverent attitude and including the resurrection. It was then rapidly followed very irreverently by Monty Python's *Life of Brian*, which used exactly the same staging as Zeffirelli, in which Brian is a character who is *not* Jesus. The film makes it absolutely clear that it is about someone like Jesus but who gets it wrong all the time. John Cleese, one of the creative team behind the film, said at the time that they just couldn't make fun of somebody as good as Jesus, so they had to show somebody trying to do the things he does and getting them wrong.

There was a lot of controversy over Denys Arcand's *Jesus of Montreal* (1989) and Martin Scorsese's *The Last Temptation of Christ* (1988). Scorsese's film is a treatment of an original Greek novel by Nikos Kazantzakis. It focuses on Jesus' struggle with the temptation just to have an ordinary life — a wife, children, sex, home and so on — and shows him fantasizing about those possibilities even on the cross. Arcand gives an account of a modern passion play set in Montreal which leads to conflict between the actor playing Jesus and the religious leaders and city authorities. More recently Murray Watts and Channel 4/S4C produced *The Miracle Maker* — a film animation with Ralph Fiennes as the voice of Jesus, Julie Christie as Mary, and Miranda Richardson as Mary Magdalene. It played in UK cinemas for several months during the summer of 2000 and was the TV movie for Easter in the UK and the United States for the first couple of years of the third millennium.

Many other films, while having no explicit reference to Jesus, explore related themes. George Lucas' *Star Wars* films (1977, 1980, 1983, 1999 and 2002) pick up on the battle between good and evil, the good side of the Force and the bad side of the Force, and the importance of self-sacrifice. Steven Spielberg's *E.T.: The Extra-Terrestrial* (1982, 2002) is about a person who comes down from above, is only understood by children, is opposed by the authorities, dies and is revived when somebody says that they love him, then reascends back into heaven. The film *The Matrix* (Warner, 1999) similarly uses a lot of motifs of Jesus in the way in which Neo is described as 'The One' and fights against evil with a woman called Trinity, even leading to his death with a resurrection and ascension at the end.

So 2,000 years after this wandering Jewish teacher, there still are huge numbers of differing interpretations being put forward. How does this Jesus, who is so fascinating to people even now, fit in with what we know of Jesus then? Let's take a look at the traditional Christian view.

Jesus Then: The Traditional Christian View

How Have Christians Traditionally Regarded Jesus?

The traditional Christian view of Jesus is that he is divine and human, or God incarnate (which means 'made flesh'); in less formal terms, Jesus is God come to earth. This is the position which went almost unchallenged as orthodox Christian teaching from the fourth to the sixteenth century (when some radicals began to deny it), and is still maintained today by the main Christian churches, including the Roman Catholic and Orthodox Churches, the churches of the sixteenth-century Reformation including the Church of England and Anglican communion, and modern evangelical, charismatic, and pentecostal churches.

There are, of course, alternative views of Jesus among people who call themselves Christians (including some members of the churches just listed), and we will be exploring some of these views later on; but for the moment, it is the traditional view which is the focus of our interest. This view is clearly expressed in the sixteenth-century language of the Church of England's Thirty-Nine Articles, article 2, which states in terms which would be acceptable to most orthodox Christians: 'The Son, which is the Word of the Father, begotten from everlasting of the Father, the very and eternal God, and of one substance with the Father, took Man's nature in the womb of the blessed Virgin, of her substance: so that two whole and perfect natures, that is to say, the Godhead and Manhood, were joined together in one person, never to be divided.' How did this view originate in early Christian teaching?

The Impact of Jesus on the Early Church

When the first Christians, as they reflected on their experience in the early days of the Church, began to consider the question of who Jesus was, it was not just his teaching that impressed them, or the quality of

6

his life, or his miracles, or even the fact that he had died as a martyr, the victim of a conspiracy between the Jewish religious authorities and the occupying Roman power. What was central to all early Christian accounts of the significance of Jesus was the fact that he had been raised from death by God on the third day after his crucifixion.

'But God raised him up', says Peter in Acts 2.24 after summarizing Jesus' life in terms of his miracles and crucifixion, 'having freed him from death, because it was impossible for him to be held in its power' (NRSV). Without the resurrection, there would be no significant story of Jesus to tell — no Christian movement and no question of Jesus for us to consider nearly two thousand years later. Whatever we believe the concept of resurrection actually means — whether physical resurrection is possible, and, if so, what actually happened when Jesus was raised and his tomb (according to the Gospel accounts) found empty — it is a fact that it was the earliest Christians' experience of Jesus as risen, a living and present figure, which launched the Christian Church.

However, belief in Jesus' resurrection alone would not entail belief in his divine status. To explain why Christians came to believe that Jesus was God as well as human, we need to look at other factors.

As Christianity grew, it rapidly expanded beyond its original geographical context in Jewish Palestine and into the Greco-Roman world — the area, particularly around the Eastern Mediterranean, which was dominated by a Greek-speaking literary, artistic, and intellectual culture (the latter expressed through a long tradition of writings in philosophy, history, medicine, and science). Many converts to Christianity looked at Jesus through the lens of Greco-Roman culture, and they would have applied to Jesus some of the cultural concepts with which they were familiar for expressing religious devotion or ideas.

The Divine Man or Saviour

One of these concepts was the 'divine man' or 'saviour', who comes from heaven to offer to people on earth some form of salvation or rescue from earthly and temporal life. Interpretation of Jesus as a divine man would make it easier to see him not only as a moral and spiritual teacher and martyr whose resurrection marked his approval by God but as someone who even during his earthly life had been a heavenly, supernatural figure.

7

> **Saviour**: a figure, often of heavenly origin, whose life or teaching offers religious fulfilment or salvation, usually understood in terms of rescue from death or sinfulness.
>
> (See Luke 2.11; John 4.42; 2 Timothy 1.10)

New Testament scholars disagree about the extent to which the figure of Jesus, as we read about his life in the Gospels, was modelled on the myth of a divine man or saviour from heaven, and whether this affects in any way the truth of the claims made by Christians for Jesus' uniqueness as the source of revelation from God. It is not clear, indeed, to what extent the myth of the divine man was ever applied to a *historical* figure apart from Jesus. (The best candidate is the first- or second-century pagan miracle worker Apollonius of Tyana, whose biography by Philostratus seems to portray him deliberately as a pagan rival to Jesus.)

> **Myth**: a story told in historical terms but really intended to convey an important spiritual or theological truth.
>
> **Pagan**: term used to refer to the traditional religious cults and myths of the Greco-Roman world.

It does seem clear, however, that Jesus came to be interpreted in these terms by Christians of Greek or Roman religious background. In other words, the idea of Jesus as a more-than-human saviour probably came to be established more easily among Christians of Greco-Roman than Jewish culture.

Worship of Jesus

Along with this goes the idea of the risen Jesus as an object of worship. It would have been natural for a Jesus who was regarded in the way just described to be actively worshipped by Christians from a Greek or Roman background. But even without Greco-Roman influence, there were pressures at work on Christians to worship the risen Jesus.

He was the Lord (cf. Luke 24.3; John 20.28, 21.7; Acts 7.59) who was the centre of their religious life and belief, active in the lives of Christians, performing miracles, supporting them in their troubles, and offering them both present and future salvation, which could be obtained by no other means than through him (cf. Acts 3.12-13). Even among Jewish Christians, belief in Jesus' divine status, during his earthly life as well as after the resurrection, would not have been long delayed. The worship of Jesus and belief in his divinity, however, would have posed real problems for Christians who were brought up in the monotheistic religious environment of Judaism. How could someone who had lived a human life be treated as divine, as the object of worship?

It was this tension between their inherited beliefs (which were also, of course, accepted by Greek and Roman Christians when they were converted) and the experiential demands of their faith in Jesus which forced Christians to begin to think more conceptually about who Jesus was, and thus led to the development of the doctrines of the Trinity and the incarnation over the early centuries of the Church.

The Origins of the Doctrines of the Trinity and the Incarnation

The doctrine of the Trinity holds that the Son of God is one of a Trinity of divine persons — Father, Son, and Holy Spirit. The doctrine of the incarnation teaches that, as he lived on earth, Jesus was not simply a human being, but the Son of God made flesh.

God's Son

Belief that Jesus was, in a special way, God's Son, was part of the common currency of early Christian thinking, but as with the resurrection this in itself would not necessarily imply Jesus' divinity, for 'Son of God' could easily be used as an honorific title for one who was God's human agent or messenger, rewarded by God with a position at God's right hand in heaven after his earthly life (cf. Mark 14.62; Acts 2.33). But, as

9

noted already, early Christians had good reasons, based on their experience of the risen Jesus, for speaking of him as divine; what they needed to help them develop this belief into a system of doctrine was a conceptual tool or piece of theological terminology which would enable them to think about Jesus as divine without denying the unity and uniqueness of God which was their Jewish heritage.

God's Word

In second-century Christianity, this conceptual tool was found in the idea of Jesus as God's Word (in Greek, *Logos*). This is a term which occurs with reference to Jesus in the New Testament (John 1.1, 14), but it would not have become such an important concept in Christian thought if it had not also been familiar to Greek philosophy (so once again, the Greco-Roman cultural context of early Christianity turns out to be important). In contemporary philosophy (particularly Middle Platonism) the Logos was understood as the means by which the transcendent God (or, in more philosophical terms, the One or supreme Mind) was related to the world. The world came into being through the Logos and also by the Logos was ordered and governed in accordance with God's providence.

Middle Platonism: school of philosophy, influential from the first century BCE to the second century CE, which emphasized the transcendence of God.

Transcendent: term used to refer to God which shows that he is not just another being in the world but entirely distinct from it and, unlike the world, by nature eternal and unchanging.

Providence: God's care for the world, by which he brings both the world as a whole and individual human beings to fulfil the purpose for which he created them.

In the New Testament, ideas which fitted well with the identification of Jesus with God's Word (as this term was understood in contemporary philosophy) are found in John 1, in Paul (1 Cor. 8.6), in the letters to the Colossians (1.15 — if this is not also by Paul), and in Hebrews (1.2), all of which speak of Jesus as the one through whom God created the world. This shows that the idea of God's Son as a heavenly figure who shared God's eternity and assisted him in the task of creation before later becoming incarnate in Jesus was not simply imported into Christian thinking from philosophy.

Loss of Simplicity

Nevertheless, to some extent, identifying Jesus with God's creative and sustaining Word inevitably meant a move away from thinking about him in terms of a personal response to the figure presented in the Gospels or to the risen Lord of the Church, to thinking about him in more abstract, conceptual terms. This move in a philosophical direction has appeared to many people, especially since the eighteenth century, as a regrettable loss of simplicity and spontaneity in Christian thinking about Jesus. However, without it, orthodox Christian thinkers from the second to the fifth centuries would have found it difficult to articulate their faith in Jesus as both divine and human at all. (In Chapter 8 we shall be looking in more detail at the doctrine of Jesus as God's Logos or Word in the early Church, and also at some less orthodox alternatives to it.)

The Formal Statement of the Doctrines of the Trinity and the Incarnation

Only in the fourth and fifth centuries was the traditional view of Jesus as God incarnate defined in terms which all Christians were, in theory, required to accept. The most important landmarks in this process are the church councils which met at Nicaea (325 CE) and Chalcedon (451 CE) — cities in Asia Minor and therefore in the heartland of Greek-speaking Christianity.

The Council of Nicaea

The Council of Nicaea was the first general council of the Christian Church (or, more accurately, of Christian bishops who were summoned to it by the Roman emperor Constantine). The purpose of the council was not to proclaim the doctrine of the Trinity as if this was something that was not already believed by Christians: it was to clarify the meaning of the doctrine in order to exclude what were perceived as unorthodox or heretical interpretations of it. Specifically, the council attacked the view of the theologian Arius that the Son of God, although a pre-existent being who had come to earth in Jesus, was in fact a creature rather than a Son born of God the Father's own divine being. Against this view, the council stated that the Son of God is 'of one substance' with the Father — in other words that the divinity of Jesus (as God's Son incarnate) and the Father are identical in quality, and that the two persons (the council of Nicaea did not say much about the person of the Holy Spirit beyond affirming belief in him) are united in substance, nature, and power.

The Council of Chalcedon

Nicaea defined the relationship of Jesus, as Son of God, to the Father, but left undefined the question of how Jesus should be understood to be both God and human. During the fourth and fifth centuries, various views continued to be held, including (among a minority of theologians) the view that Jesus was not, strictly, a human being at all. But at the Council of Chalcedon, limits were set to what it was permissable for orthodox Christians to believe about Jesus. The council defined the relationship of the divine nature of Jesus to his humanity in terms which have generally been accepted by Christians ever since: Jesus is recognized as being 'in two natures', divine and human, which come together into one person.

The language of this definition, and of the Council of Nicaea, is philosophical, in that terms like 'substance', 'nature', and 'person' are common in the vocabulary of Greek philosophy. They need to be carefully interpreted and understood if the truth (as orthodox Christians see it) behind the inherently paradoxical claim that the same individual, Jesus, could be both the divine Son of God and a human being is to be grasped. The Councils of Nicaea and Chalcedon defined orthodox Christian belief, but intellectual debate and attempts at closer definition have continued, often based on fresh investigation of the way in which belief in Jesus' divine-and-human status came to be established in the early Church, or on the adoption of new theological perspectives of the sort which we will begin to examine later in this chapter.

Reinterpreting Jesus

The Religious Debate

So the range of views and debates about the person of Jesus now is nothing new. Right from the start, discussion raged about who he was or is and what his life and death signified. Such debates led to the writing of the New Testament during the first century and continued through the next few centuries leading to the definitions of the incarnation and of the Trinity. Nor are these debates about the interpretation of Jesus confined just to Christians — they affect all the world's main religious traditions, and also generate debates outside the Church at both academic and popular levels.

Prior to the Jewish War of 70 CE Christians were seen as one group within Judaism. The Jews comprised many different groups, with different beliefs, who all practised the Jewish religion. Only the Pharisees and the Jewish Christians survived the war and the destruction of Jerusalem, becoming the dominant force in the reconstruction of rabbinic Judaism. From this point on, the parting of the ways between rabbinic Judaism and the early Church became inevitable, while other groups such as the Essenes and the Sadducees perished.

These discussions have continued from the New Testament period down to today, with many Jewish scholars working on New Testament books and the person of Jesus. Some see him as a teacher or rabbi — like other rabbis of the period such as Rabbi Hillel — but not as God incarnate. On the other hand, because of the tragic history of Jewish-Christian relations, this is a very sensitive issue for other Jews who would firmly state that 'Jesus is nothing to do with Judaism'.

For Muslims, Jesus is revered as a prophet, following on from Abraham, Isaac and Moses. They accept that he was the son of Mary by virgin birth (Qur'an Sura 19.30-40), and have no problems with his teaching and healing ministry. However, they believe that he did not die on the cross but instead it was only a likeness of him (Sura 4.156-59). Je-

13

Jewish Groups at the Time of Jesus

1. The **Sadducees** were mostly aristocrats in Jerusalem, co-operating with the Romans; they were linked to the chief priests and active in the temple with its sacrifices and cult; their spirituality was centred on the Pentateuch, the first five books of the Scriptures, and they did not believe in the resurrection after death.

2. The **Pharisees** were a mostly non-priestly renewal movement, trying to interpret all the scriptures, as well as the oral traditions; they believed in the resurrection and the importance of purity laws; they would be found in synagogues and communities across the country.

3. The **Essenes** included both priests and lay people, with particularly strict views about the temple and purity; as exclusivists, many withdrew into desert communities like Qumran, where they produced the Dead Sea Scrolls.

4. For others, their 'zeal' for Jewish Law and belief led not to withdrawal but to active armed resistance against the Romans; some of these were called **Zealots**, while others were *sicarii*, dagger-carriers, or what we might term 'freedom fighters'.

---

sus is treated with great respect, as is seen from time to time when Muslims protest at blasphemies to which Christians seem to be resigned. The doctrines of the incarnation and the Trinity, however, are seen as a fundamental denial of monotheism and therefore totally unacceptable to Muslims.

Jesus is revered as a teacher in other faiths, such as Sikhism and Hinduism, where he would be placed alongside other religious teachers. Humanists — those who claim not to believe — still talk of Jesus as a great moral teacher.

Revising Understandings

Down the ages, thinkers have continued to re-create Jesus in their own image, from Jesus as Renaissance man to Jesus as nineteenth-century liberal. In the nineteenth century various 'lives of Jesus' were written. One of the earliest examples was by Ernest Renan who viewed the Gospels as 'legendary biographies' from which he constructed his somewhat romantic *Life of Jesus* (1863).

> **Apocalyptic**: from the Greek for 'to reveal' or 'unveil'; used for literature which reveals the veiled hand of God behind events in human history, common in Judaism in the centuries before and around the birth of Jesus. Hence Apocalypse is another name for the book of Revelation.

Soon after that we see the development of the 'social gospel', where Jesus' teaching of the Kingdom of God is interpreted and applied for the general improvement of the human condition, both in terms of the well-being of the individual and in a corporate sense. This contrasts very strongly with the apocalyptic and eschatological interpretation that sees Jesus as a Jewish prophet of the end of the world, and puts the emphasis not on human effort but on divine intervention, stressing the Kingdom coming in glory with a great cataclysm.

> **Eschatology**: the study of the end times or 'last days', from the Greek *eschatos,* meaning last or final.

Then in the twentieth century, Jesus the revolutionary became fashionable. The stress here was on liberation and a whole school of thought was developed by the name of 'liberation theology'. In this setting there was prolonged debate about whether Jesus himself approved the use of arms against the Romans — and whether arms could be used by Christians in the liberation struggles in South America or Southern Africa.

The Quest for the Historical Jesus

It is usually held that the so-called quest for the historical Jesus was started by H. S. Reimarus (1694-1768) who discovered the 'real' Jesus as a failed Jewish revolutionary, rather than the divine figure which his first disciples produced for the founding of the Church. Similar reconstructions followed from the likes of D. F. Strauss, H. J. Holtzmann and J. Weiss, coming to a head in Albert Schweitzer's depiction of Jesus as an apocalyptic prophet.

Such studies attempted to get 'behind' the Gospels to the Jesus of history — and away from the Christ of faith and the traditional Christology of the Church, as we shall see in Chapter 2.

The Quest for the Popular Jesus

Rightly acclaimed for his biographies of Tolstoy and C. S. Lewis, A. N. Wilson turned his attention to Jesus in his book *Jesus* (1992). Drawing on some recent Jesus scholarship (but missing other parts), Wilson reconstructs Jesus' origins and personal development as a Jewish teacher, but rejects the claim that Jesus was the founder of the Christian Church, instead seeing Paul as the real founder of a church which would have been quite alien to Jesus.

Another reconstruction of Jesus made a lot of headlines for Barbara Thiering, who worked on a method of so-called 'decoding' the Dead Sea Scrolls (*Jesus the Man*, 1992).

Dead Sea Scrolls: parchment or papyrus scrolls discovered in caves by the Dead Sea between 1947 and 1956; written in Hebrew, Aramaic and Greek by a Jewish religious community from c. 150 BCE until destroyed by the Romans in 68 CE.

From this decoding she produces a story about Jesus involved in a power struggle in the Qumran community, his marriage to Mary Magdalene (and their three children) and his subsequent divorce to marry Lydia of Philippi. As an example of this 'decoding', we find in the book of Acts (16.14) a phrase which says 'the Lord opened the heart of Lydia' — which, in traditional interpretation, means she had a spiritual revelation. However, in Thiering's reinterpretation, 'the Lord opened the heart of Lydia' means that Jesus divorced Mary Magdalene and got married to Lydia. Far-fetched as this may seem, Barbara Thiering went on a lot of chat shows, sold hundreds of thousands of copies of hardback books, and made a huge amount of money.

Intriguingly, Sir Arthur C. Clarke, writer of *2001: A Space Odyssey* and Fellow of King's College, London, in his science-fiction novel, *The Light of Other Days* (Arthur C. Clarke with Stephen Baxter, 2000), included a whole biography of Jesus, in which by using worm-hole cameras going back through time people try to reconstruct and film Jesus. Again it is interesting that as a committed atheist, Clarke is fascinated by the person of Jesus at the start of the third millennium.

The Current Academic Debate about Jesus

At the risk of oversimplification, the current debate can be polarized in two ways, between those who put Jesus in a Greek philosophical background and those who put him within the background of first-century Palestinian Judaism.

The first view is represented by John Dominic Crossan and by the 'Jesus Seminar', chaired by Robert Funk. They see Jesus as a philosophical teacher of Greek wisdom, and put the blame on Mark and the Gospel writers for inventing the Jewish myth of Jesus. The most recent book to emerge from the Jesus Seminar is *Five Gospels,* an edition of the four canonical Gospels plus the Gospel of Thomas. What caught media attention was the colour coding in which the text was produced, which we will examine in more detail later.

The second school of thought stresses Jesus' Jewish background, with a lot of argument on the historicity of the Gospels. In the next chapter we will consider this aspect, exemplified by the works of Geza Vermes, E. P. Sanders and N. T. Wright.

All in all, this is a huge area of debate, with vast numbers of books being produced and conferences convened, trying to understand how we are to interpret Jesus today.

Reinterpreting the Tradition

The traditional teaching about Jesus, divine and human, has been subject to a number of challenges in Western religious thought in the period since the sixteenth and particularly the eighteenth centuries. Jesus has often been reinterpreted, and understandings of his person have been put forward which are not as dependent as orthodox Christian teaching on the theological tradition of the early Church which was crystallized in the doctrines of the Councils of Nicaea and Chalcedon.

This reinterpretation has not been confined to non-Christians who are interested in Jesus (although many who would not call themselves Christians have been fascinated with his life and teaching), or to the fringes of the churches or popular movements of protest against them — though these have certainly played a part. Some well-informed theologians with a strong commitment to the Christian gospel and to biblical teaching have also been moved to question the traditional view.

For example, the great British scientist Sir Isaac Newton (1642-1727), who wrote numerous theological as well as scientific works, denied the doctrine of the Trinity, and influenced a number of Anglican writers of the early eighteenth century, most notably Samuel Clarke (1675-1729), author of *The Scripture-Doctrine of the Trinity* (1712), and William Whiston (1667-1752), Newton's successor as professor of Mathematics at Cambridge University, who left the Church of England after being led by his study of the early Church to embrace the beliefs of Arius.

All of these scholars and others like them were led to their unorthodox conclusions by the new emphasis of the eighteenth-century Enlightenment on empirical historical research and the application of practical (as opposed to abstract philosophical) reasoning to religious questions. In the later eighteenth and nineteenth centuries these trends

---

The Enlightenment: a movement of thought in eighteenth-century Europe which emphasized research, observation, and scientific experiment rather than the authority of religious tradition or abstract metaphysical speculation.

---

in Western thought caused many scholars to question not only the traditional doctrines about Jesus, but also the historical reliability of the Gospel portrait of Jesus as a supernatural figure, a miracle worker who was raised from the dead.

The Twentieth Century

For many critics of the traditional doctrine, the fact that it is expressed in terms drawn from the philosophy of the Greco-Roman world is one of its most significant weaknesses. Terms such as 'substance' or 'being' and 'nature' (the inherent qualities of a substance) are no longer used by philosophers with the same technical meanings as they bore in ancient Greek. Should Christians continue to be bound by this system of thought in expressing their beliefs about Jesus?

Many twentieth-century theologians, including some of the most influential, thought that both the terminology and the ideas of Greek philosophy should be abandoned. For example, the German New Testament scholar Rudolf Bultmann (1884-1976) believed that Christians should refuse to make any metaphysical claims about the person of Jesus, or assert any but the most minimal belief in the historical facts of his life; they should express their faith in terms of an encounter with or decision for Jesus as God's revelation (concepts drawn from existentialist philosophy). The Swiss theologian Karl Barth (1886-1968) did not go as far as Bultmann in rejecting traditional doctrines, but he attempted to disengage the concept of Jesus as God's Word from philosophy, and reassert the primacy of God's revelation in the Bible over philosophical concepts and arguments such as those which influenced the theologians of the early Church.

Existentialism: a twentieth-century philosophical movement characterized by a focus on personal experience of 'authentic existence' rather than objective metaphysical arguments about divine or human nature.

Radical Christianity

The work of theologians since the eighteenth century has led many Christians to wonder whether it may in fact be possible to maintain a Christian faith without belief in the doctrines of the Trinity and the incarnation. May not Jesus be believed in and revered by Christians as a religious teacher who was inspired by God, without being the subject of large-scale metaphysical claims such as that he is 'of one substance' with the Father? Should all modern accounts of Christianity, including new hymns, forms of prayer, and doctrinal statements agreed by the various churches, necessarily incorporate the traditional doctrines in their original form? The Church of England bishop John Robinson (1919-83) famously caused a major controversy with his book *Honest to God* (1963), which popularized a number of radical theological views including those of Bultmann, and argued for a reconstruction of Christian thought on the grounds that speaking of God as a transcendent 'person' made little sense to twentieth-century Christians, and should be replaced with a doctrine of God as an immanent 'ground of being' and of Jesus as the one who most fully expressed, in his life, the relationship of human beings to this ground or source of meaning and value. And there have been many other theologians in the last generation who have developed equally radical views.

Nevertheless, the traditional doctrines retain their vitality in the shaping of modern Christian thought and continue to be accepted by the majority of theologians in the various Christian traditions; along with more radical theological concepts, as well as popular perceptions of Jesus as a superstar, a prophet, a revolutionary, or the inspiration for Hollywood movies, they continue both to supply answers to the question 'Who is Jesus?', and to demand further questioning and exploration. In the following chapters we shall look in more detail at Jesus in the New Testament and the evidence for him, and at the beliefs about him which developed in the early Church. The final chapter will return to some of the questions raised here about the value of the traditional Christian doctrines about Jesus and about his significance for us today.

THE NEW TESTAMENT

The Historical Jesus

In the last chapter we caught something of the importance of Jesus *now*, in our culture today, and looked at some of the different interpretations people are making of what seemed to be, even then in his own time, an enigmatic figure. Behind the Jesus worshipped in churches by millions all over the world, and the flower-power figure of Jesus Christ Superstar, can there really be one person? And what can we know about the historical reality of Jesus *then*, someone who lived so long ago and has been understood in such different ways over the centuries which lie between us? To answer these questions, in this chapter we need to dig down into the past, and then try to build up a picture of what we can know about Jesus.

Digging Down: Quests for the Historical Jesus

Let us look at some of the work that has been done to find out what we can know about the historical Jesus of Nazareth.

The Quest for the Historical Jesus in the Eighteenth and Nineteenth Centuries

It is generally agreed that the search for the historical Jesus was set in motion by H. S. Reimarus (1694-1768). He argued that you couldn't just read the Gospels as a factual narrative; you had to take into account that the Gospels were written by believers, who wanted to see Jesus as a divine figure, and had written the Gospels to prove the point. The 'real' Jesus, he concluded, was a failed Jewish revolutionary who was promoting the Kingdom of God, but whose revolution didn't succeed and who was therefore crucified.

This attempt to separate what became known as 'the Jesus of history' from 'the Christ of faith' motivated a quest which grew in importance over the next couple of centuries and inspired a great host of writers and theologians, many of whom came out of the German liberal Protestant tradition, and who sought to apply the critical methods of historical research to the search for Jesus.

Of course, the problem is that the only way to discover the Jesus of history is through the documents of the Gospels and a few other contemporary documents which we will consider shortly. If you then strip out from these the aspects of Jesus which you find uncongenial, you have a slim and conveniently flexible base on which to build. The results have been quite varied, from Jesus the nineteenth-century liberal and Jesus the armed revolutionary to Jesus the hairy prophet of the end of the world.

Apocalyptic literature: writings which 'take away the veil' so we see God's purposes, especially in relation to the end of the world.

A hugely important book in this debate was Albert Schweitzer's *The Quest for the Historical Jesus* which was published in Germany in 1906. He worked through all the issues and postulated a Jesus who was a prophet of the end times. A great many apocalyptic writings were around in Jesus' period, and Schweitzer said that he fitted into this pattern, that he was a prophet who preached the coming end. The Kingdom of God, according to Schweitzer, was not actually a revolution, but was about something God himself would do at the end of all time.

All these studies intended to get behind the Gospels, as it were, away from a traditional Christology which was the understanding of the Church, to a Jesus of history.

Early Studies on the Historical Jesus

H. S. Reimarus: *Von dem Zwecke Jesu und seiner Jünger* (Braunschweig, 1778).

D. F. Strauss: *Das Leben Jesu kritisch bearbeitet* (Tübingen, 1835); English translation: *The Life of Jesus Critically Examined* (London: Chapman, 1846; SCM Press, 1972).

H. J. Holtzmann: *Die synoptischen Evangelien: Ihr Ursprung und geschichtlicher Charakter* (Leipzig, 1863).

J. Weiss: *Die Predigt Jesu vom Reiche Gottes* (Göttingen, 1900); English translation: *Jesus' Proclamation of the Kingdom of God* (London: SCM Press, 1971).

A. Schweitzer: *Geschichte der Leben-Jesu-Forschung* (Tübingen, 1906); English translation: *The Quest of the Historical Jesus* (London: A. & C. Black, 1954).

Critics of the Early Twentieth Century (1900-1950)

When we talk of criticizing the Gospels, we don't mean it in the negative sense: 'How dare you criticize me!' Criticism in this sense means 'analysis', looking at a question in terms of academic debate which can be both a positive and a negative evaluation.

Textual Criticism

During the early part of the twentieth century, the Gospel critics were involved in two areas of study. The first was the history of the text of the Gospels. We don't have any of the original manuscripts of the Gospels, just as we don't have the original manuscripts of any ancient works. What we rely on as texts are actually copies of copies of copies. As a classicist I have studied and taught Latin and Greek literature, and I know that for many of even the major classical works such as those of Thucydides and Tacitus, we have only a few manuscripts which were copied many centuries after they were first written, and in some cases nearly a thousand years later. What is remarkable about the Gospels is that we have literally hundreds of early copies of the texts, only a century or so after they were first written. So textual criticism is the research which tries to get back to the text exactly as it was first written. When you look at English translations of the Gospels today you can be sure that you are reading a very reliable text, which has been translated with the confidence that this is what the first authors wrote.

Source Criticism

The second field of study which made great headway in the early part of the twentieth century was source criticism, which is the question of how the Gospels relate to one another. In particular, if you look at Mark, Matthew and Luke you see fairly rapidly that they have many of the same stories, and in fact they use much of the same material which was handed down to them by oral tradition. Something over 95 per cent of Mark's Gospel is repeated in Matthew and Luke. Matthew and Luke are both quite a lot longer than Mark, nearly twice as long, but they use all of Mark's material and weave in a lot of other material. There are also some passages which Matthew and Luke have in common, but which don't come from Mark: this suggests there was another document which they both had but which is no longer known. This has been designated 'Q' by theologians (from the German word *Quelle*, meaning 'source'), and the now generally accepted explanation of the relationships between the Gospels can be seen in Figure 1 (on p. 27).

We sometimes see the same process at work when marking students' essays. No student is so crass as to copy an essay from a text-book or off the internet, because they know they won't get away with it — and copying is a severe offence today. However, in the ancient world, it was often seem as a compliment, paying deference to a previous writer as your authority — and this is how Matthew and Luke use Mark as their guiding narrative. However, someone today can read a text-book, make notes on it, and then later copy the notes into the essay, which is very tempting if it sounds convincing or especially if they haven't really understood it in the first place. So when I come to mark the essay, I suddenly hit a passage which sounds familiar, and think 'Oh, yes, I know where that comes from.' In the same way you can be reading Matthew or Luke and come across something that sounds familiar from the other Gospel — in

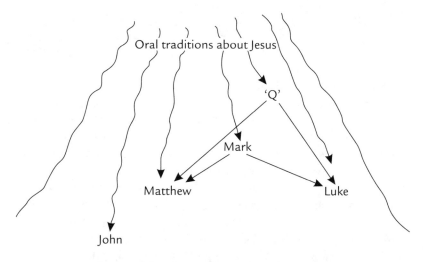

**Figure 1. The consensus explanation of the
relationships of the gospels**

other words, it is taken from their shared source, 'Q'. Tracking down the
relationships between the texts is the subject of source criticism.

John seems to have used quite different sources from the other
three, and whatever overlap there is (about 10 per cent) would be explained by oral traditions reaching the writer quite independently. Matthew, Mark and Luke are known as the Synoptic Gospels.

> **Synoptic**: from the Greek, meaning 'to look at something to-
> gether'.

You can look at the three of them together and compare and contrast them. By doing that, and looking at the different ways in which Jesus' words are phrased in them, you can begin a process of 'peeling off'
the layers of interpretation. Because Matthew and Luke were written
later than Mark, you can ask, 'Why have Matthew and Luke, who have
written with a particular focus of interest, used Mark's material, which
was written from his own viewpoint?' In this way you can try to get back
to the original sayings of the historical Jesus.

Form Criticism

Rudolph Bultmann was mentioned in the last chapter as the theologian who brought an existential dimension to our understanding of Jesus. He was also the New Testament critic who developed what we now know as 'form criticism'.

Form criticism looks at the Gospels as a group of stories and asks, 'What is their form, or type?' One form would be parables, another healing stories, and a third would be stories of conflict between Jesus and the people of his day. By analysing these forms, we can see how these stories would have been passed down the oral tradition. If we look at the opening chapters of Mark, we see the healing of a leper in 1.40-45 followed by other snippets, many of them about healing. The stories of conflict and controversy appear together in 2.1-12, 13-17, 18-22, 23-28 and 3.1-6. In chapter 4 is a collection of parables about the Kingdom of God. It looks as though Mark has fitted together pieces of oral tradition in recognizable categories.

To say that stories were passed down by word of mouth is not to suggest that it was a totally haphazard affair. Many ancient texts, such as the poems of Homer — the *Iliad* and *Odyssey* — were passed down orally for four or five centuries before they were written down. The corresponding period for the Gospels is very brief — actually about a generation. The first Gospel was written down in about the 60s, thirty years after Jesus, and the other three were written during the 70s, 80s and 90s. This is quite a short period. And of course the ancient world was much more used to memorizing in this way and accuracy was a high priority: the oral tradition actually preserved the original in a very clear way.

The New Quest for the Historical Jesus (1950-1975)

In October 1953 a pupil of Rudolph Bultmann called Ernst Käsemann gave a lecture entitled 'The New Quest for the Historical Jesus'. In this, he agreed with Bultmann that the Gospels were not a form of biography of Jesus, but said it was still necessary to analyse the link between the Jesus of history, Jesus himself, and the early Church's understanding of him, and their preaching and teaching of him as the Messiah, the Christ.

Messiah or **Christ**: Messiah is a Hebrew word, and Christ is
Greek: they both mean 'the anointed One' — the person who
has been anointed by God.

So the 'New Quest' got under way in the 1950s and 1960s. The question they were asking was, 'How do we know, when Jesus says something in the Gospels, whether he actually said it or someone else has put the words into his mouth?' In their search back through the Gospels to get to the historical Jesus they came up with several 'criteria of authenticity'.

Criteria of Authenticity

- The first they called *dissimilarity*. If what Jesus is saying is dissimilar to what the Jewish tradition and the early Church was saying, then it can only come from Jesus himself.
- Then there was *multiple attestation,* when Jesus says the same thing, or the same sort of thing via different witnesses, in different Gospels or writings. For example, he talks about 'the Kingdom of God' just about everywhere, so it is likely that this concept can be tracked back to the historical Jesus.
- Another criterion was *unintentionality.* An example of this is when Jesus says that he doesn't know when the end of time will be (Mark 13.32). The early Church wanted to show that Jesus knows everything, so it's very unintentional — that is to say the early Church would never make up the fact — that Jesus admits he doesn't know something.
- These critics were also looking for *coherence* — how all the sayings fitted together.
- They even considered whether certain phrases could be *translated* back into ancient Aramaic, although it's quite likely that Jesus also spoke Greek.

These tools were used quite a lot in the 1960s to produce evidence for the life of the historical Jesus. The problem with this is that you end up with a Jesus who is somehow vacuum-packed — dissimilar from what went before in his own culture, and dissimilar from what was being taught in the early Church. In fact we all exist within a culture, and that concept had been lost along the way. So these methods began to run into difficulties.

The Titles of Jesus

Another aspect of the quest during these years was an attempt to understand Jesus in terms of the various titles that were used of him. In the texts, he is often called a 'prophet'. Since the early Church believed that Jesus is a lot more than a prophet, it's quite significant that the stories refer to him as a prophet: that may well reflect how people saw him in his own day. Equally, he's also regularly called 'Rabbi' or 'Teacher'. So the argument would run that probably most people listening to Jesus thought of him as some kind of wandering prophet or teacher figure, and we know that there were a lot of these teaching their way around Israel or Palestine at that time.

- The word *Christ,* or 'Messiah', means the 'anointed One of God', and that's used of Jesus in nearly every New Testament book. That doesn't mean to say that Jesus goes around saying 'I am the Christ: pleased to meet you, what's your name?' It is the phrase that's used to describe him, particularly used when people express their faith in him and especially later in the Gospels.
- The name that Jesus likes to use of himself regularly in the Synoptic Gospels is *Son of Man.* This is a phrase, *bar nash* in Hebrew or Aramaic, which is a way of referring to somebody in a slightly impersonal way. It is like the word 'one' we have in English but 'one' is only used by people like the royal family. 'One has to earn one's crust, doesn't one?' is a way of saying 'I have to' without using the word 'I'. However, in German you have the word *man* and in French you have *on* and these are not so exclusive. The phrase 'son of Man' is a bit like that: an oblique way of referring to yourself, but the 'son of Man' is also the way of describing a human being. In the Old Testament writings, the Hebrew Scriptures, the figure of the 'son of Man' appears regularly as a representative human being who is sent by God to bring God's message to the people (Ezek. 12.2; Dan. 7.1-14).

- The word *Lord* is used particularly in the rest of the New Testament as an expression of belief in Jesus as Lord and God. A Jew will not say the name of God, so if he is reading in synagogue, and the name of God appears in the text, he will always say 'the Lord' rather than reading the divine name. So when Jesus is described as 'Lord' in the rest of the New Testament, it is a way of saying that he is equivalent to God (Acts 2.36; Phil. 2.11). He's also called 'Lord' quite a bit in the Gospels, but the problem is that in normal parlance, the word 'Lord' was also a way of saying, 'Sir', or 'Master' — a term of respect, as in Mark 7.28: 'Yes, Lord', 'No, Lord'. So we have to be careful when we read the word 'Lord' in the Gospels as to whether this is a social use or a theological use.
- Lastly, let's look at the phrase *Son of God.* There is cautious use of this phrase in the Synoptic Gospels: it is used eight times in Mark, ten times in Luke and fifteen times in Matthew. John, however, states that the whole purpose of his Gospel is that the reader might believe that 'Jesus is the Christ, the Son of God' (20.31). He uses the term twenty-five times, not only as the narrator, but also with Jesus using it of himself in debate with the Jews and in his teaching. The rest of the New Testament calls Jesus 'Son of God' with great freedom.

Examining these titles, some people say you can actually follow a development of the understanding of Jesus. Jesus is seen first as a human being, a prophet or peripatetic teacher — this is known as a 'low' view of Jesus. This early understanding evolved or developed over time into belief in a quasi-divine figure that people then began calling the Messiah, Son of God and Lord — this is known as a 'high' view. This theory of development is very neat, but it doesn't actually work quite as simply as that. When we come to do a more detailed analysis of the New Testament text, we discover that the 'high' ideas of Jesus as God are used by the writers at quite an early stage, and the 'low' ideas of Jesus as prophet or teacher still occur at quite a late stage. So this developmental theory doesn't stand up to further study.

Redaction Criticism

Another development during the 1960s and 1970s was called 'redaction criticism'. *Redaktor* in German simply means a newspaper editor, and redaction criticism means editorial criticism. For instance, you could pick up a newspaper to see what happened yesterday in Parliament or Congress. If you read the report first in a conservative paper and then in a tabloid, you will find slightly different versions of it, reflecting the editorial stance of each newspaper. In the same way, as we look at the Gospels of Matthew, Mark, Luke and John, they tell the same story in different ways reflecting their editorial stance. Therefore, we need to study each Gospel in turn, and that's what we'll do in the next chapter.

Late Twentieth-Century Approaches (1975-2000)

The 'Jesus Seminar' from California

In the last chapter I mentioned briefly that the current debate about Jesus can be divided, at the risk of gross oversimplification, between two groups. The first of these we might call the Californian approach.

The 'Jesus Seminar' is a group of mostly North American academics who are using all the critical tools I have mentioned. At the end of all the debates about Jesus' sayings, the Jesus Seminar voted their way through every single saying of Jesus, and they used little coloured beads or pebbles — red, pink, grey and black. If they voted red, that meant, 'Yes, that's definitely Jesus.' Pink meant 'Well, that sounds like him.' Grey stood for 'Probably not, there's been some mistake,' and black, 'No, definitely not the historical Jesus at all.' This naturally caused a huge storm in the States, with massive TV coverage as you might expect.

The result underlined the power of an interesting phenomenon which colours every attempt to reconstruct the historical Jesus. John Dominic Crossan, one of the most famous theologians involved in the Jesus Seminar, has produced a Jesus who is not Jewish in his teaching, but more like a Greek wisdom teacher or philosopher, and he's against sexism, imperialism and all the oppressiveness of the Roman empire. In other words, he's a Californian. The nineteenth-century liberals produced a Jesus who bore a surprising similarity to a nineteenth-century liberal. Those involved in revolutionary movements, on the other hand, have put together an image of Jesus who is, amazingly, a revolutionary.

One image that has been used of trying to track down the historical Jesus is to say it is like looking down a very deep well, and seeing a face at the bottom in the water. You state 'That's the historical Jesus' when actually of course it's your own reflection staring back at you. This is a temptation for each of us, as well as for theologians, and a danger we need to guard against.

Jesus in His Jewish Context

The second movement I want to mention in the current debate about Jesus opposes the so-called 'Californian school'. This approach is known as the 'Third Quest', and it concentrates on putting Jesus into his Jewish context, that of first-century Judaism. The major figure of this movement was a Jewish scholar called Geza Vermes, who wrote a very important book in 1973 called *Jesus the Jew:* his point is an obvious one, but one that two thousand years of Christian history had seemed to have forgotten about. A tremendous reappraisal of Jesus as a Jewish rabbi and teacher has flowed from that. Two particular scholars in this regard are E. P. Sanders and N. T. Wright, mentioned in Chapter 1, who have done a great deal to restore our understanding of Jesus in his historical Jewish context.

What Wright has called the 'Third Quest' has relocated Jesus in the Judaism of his own day, following the direction set by Geza Vermes. Members of this school of thought include B. F. Meyer, A. E. Harvey and M. J. Borg. Meyer carefully distinguishes between Jesus' public proclamation of the Kingdom and his private esoteric revelation of his Messianic identity. Harvey's 1980 Bampton Lectures used the notion of 'historical constraints' to work to a non-incarnational understanding of Messiahship. Borg's analysis of the political situation suggests that Jesus' apocalyptic warnings are not directed to a divine judgement but concern the imminent catastrophe of war and destruction; as a holy sage, Jesus summoned Israel to mercy and love.

The giant of this quest is E. P. Sanders, who has transformed our understanding of Palestinian Judaism, particularly with regard to the Pharisees and attitudes to the Law, so often caricatured in Christian preaching. Beginning with Jesus' actions (particularly in the temple) rather than his sayings, Sanders places Jesus firmly within Jewish restoration eschatology and what he terms 'covenantal nomism', that is a concern for the law *(nomos)* as part of the covenant, rather than for merely legalistic purposes. However, Sanders allows that Jesus saw himself as the 'viceroy' or representative of God's Kingship.

Finally, Tom Wright set the stage for his five-volume blockbuster series on *Christian Origins and the Question of God* with the first volume in 1992 on the historical, sociological and literary background; Volume Two, *Jesus and the Victory of God,* burst upon us in 1996 to describe Jesus' place within Judaism, his aims and his Christological self-understanding — followed by Volume Three on the *Resurrection of the Son of God* in 2003, with other volumes to come.

So those are some of the attempts to dig down and find the historical Jesus, and some of the difficulties they have run into. Many of these lines of thought seem to follow a process of 'stripping away', until you wonder what is left. Some people see it like a nut, removing the outer casing to find the real kernel inside. For others it is like peeling an onion: you work your way down through the layers until there is nothing left, and the only thing you can be certain of is that there will be tears!

Building Up: Who Was Jesus?

So let's start again from a different viewpoint. What can we be reasonably certain of? Can we build Jesus back up again from first principles?

Did Jesus Actually Ever Exist?

There are those who argue that Jesus is a figment of the Church's imagination, that there never was a Jesus at all. I have to say that I do not know any respectable critical scholar who says that any more. There's a lot of evidence for his existence.

The New Testament

First, of course, we have the books of the New Testament themselves. You'll say, straight away, that they're the product of the Church, so

34

they're biased. Yes, it is true that they came from the Church, but nothing comes from nothing. Something has to happen for a story to be told, and we need somebody to start it all in the first place. So in the New Testament you have the Gospels, four books about Jesus, and a whole series of letters written by early Christians talking about the importance of Jesus. The letters are actually much earlier than the Gospels, written within the next couple of decades after Jesus. If Jesus of Nazareth had not existed as a historical person, we would have needed someone very like Jesus to be the catalyst to which they are all responding. That doesn't mean, of course, that this is necessarily the Jesus we see in the New Testament. That may be a version of the Church's interpretation, and we shall argue about that as we go.

Non-canonical Sources

> **Canon**: the official list of the books of the Bible. The Hebrew canon consists of the Hebrew Scriptures which Christians call the Old Testament, and which Jews call the Law, the Prophets and the Writings. The New Testament canon is the list of 27 books found in the New Testament.

The non-canonical books are interesting because these are the books outside the Bible — books that the Church didn't accept into the Bible, which give us interesting views of Jesus. There's a text called the 'Gospel of Thomas' which consists of 114 sayings of Jesus. There's no narrative, no story, just a list of his sayings.

Then there are what we call Jewish Christian Gospels, written by Christians who remained within Judaism when most Christians parted from the synagogue at the end of the first century and the beginning of the second. Among these are the Gospel of the Nazarenes, the Gospel of the Ebionites and the Gospel of the Hebrews. Again, they are an attempt to show how orthodox practising Jews have found the Messiah in Jesus of Nazareth. These Gospels don't exist as whole texts, but as fragments and quotations, and once again they talk about Jesus.

There are also fragments of other Gospels by groups which were seen by the rest of the Church as heretical groups, particularly philo-

---

Extracts from the Gospel of Thomas

Let him who seeks, not cease seeking until he finds, and when he finds, he will be troubled, and when he has been troubled, he will marvel and he will reign over the All. *(Saying 2)*

I took my stand in the midst of the world and in flesh I appeared to them: I found them all drunk, I found none among them athirst. And my soul was afflicted for the sons of men, because they are blind in their heart and do not see that empty they have come into the world and that empty they seek to go out of the world again. *(Saying 28)*

It is impossible for a man to mount two horses and to stretch two bows, and it is impossible for a servant to serve two masters, otherwise he will honour the one and offend the other. *(Saying 47)*

---

sophical and speculative groups. They have given us the 'Secret Gospel of Mark' and the 'Gospel of Peter'. Some of the stories are there as fragments, but again, they are similar to the stories in the canonical Gospels.

Jewish Sources

Then we move on to Jewish witnesses to the historical fact of Jesus, especially Josephus. Josephus was a Jewish historian who was actually a military leader during the Jewish rebellion, but then joined the Romans and wrote a history of the Jewish people to try to explain the Jews to the Romans. In his very important book *The Antiquities of the Jews* there are two sections in which he refers to Jesus. In XX.200 he refers to 'James, the brother of Jesus the so-called Christ'. He also refers to Jesus in a section which is greatly debated (XVIII.65ff.). He describes him as 'a wise man', says that he was a teacher of the people who won over both Jews and Greeks, and that he was crucified under Pilate and that Christians are named after him. There is a certain amount of debate about that text, because he also says a lot of positive things about Jesus that some people think are later Christian interpolations into the text. But this much is clear: he witnesses to the historical life of Jesus, that he was crucified under Pilate, that he had a group of followers and that Christians take their name from him.

Meanwhile, in the rabbinic sources after Judaism and Christianity moved apart, there are a number of accusations. For example in a Jewish tractate, *bSanhedrin* 43a, Jesus is described as a 'sorcerer who led people astray'. It says, 'On the Sabbath of the Passover Festival Jesu the Nazarene was hanged. The herald cried, "Here is Jesus the Nazarene: he has practised sorcery and led Israel to apostasy." He was then hanged on the eve of the Passover.'

Roman Sources

Jesus is also mentioned in the writings of the three main Roman historical writers from the end of the first century CE — Pliny, Tacitus and Suetonius. Cornelius Tacitus (55–c. 120) was a Roman politician who rose to be consul, the highest rank under the emperor, and then became the historian of the first century of the empire. When he is describing the fire at Rome under Nero in 64 CE, he says that it was wrongly blamed on the early Christians; he then explains that they take their name from Christ, who was executed under Pontius Pilate in Judaea, although many Christians now even live in Rome (*Annals* 15.44.3). Suetonius refers to the expulsion of Jews from Rome under the previous emperor, Claudius, in 49 CE as a result of unrest 'stirred up by Christus' (*Claud.* 25.4) — which probably refers to debate between Jewish Christians and other Jews about whether Jesus is the Christ or not.

Pliny the Younger (61–c. 120) was acting as a Roman governor in Asia Minor in around 111 CE when he wrote to the Emperor Trajan about what he discovered from people accused of being Christians.

Thus we can see that as well as the early Christian accounts, there are many sources outside the New Testament, including Roman and Jewish opponents, which all point to the fact that Jesus existed as a historical figure who went about teaching, causing controversy among his fellow Jews until he was eventually executed by a Roman governor — yet remarkably enough, many of his followers spread across the empire in the years which followed, even to Rome itself.

Pliny

They declared that the sum total of their guilt or error amounted to no more than this: they had met regularly before dawn on a fixed day to chant verses alternately amongst themselves in honour of Christ as if to a god, and also to bind themselves by oath, not for any criminal purpose, but to abstain from theft, robbery, and adultery, to commit no breach of trust and not to deny a deposit when called upon to restore it [. . .] I decided it was all the more necessary to extract the truth by torture from two slave-women, whom they call deaconesses. I found nothing but a degenerate sort of cult carried to extravagant lengths.

(Pliny, *Letters*, 10.96)

A Brief Outline of Jesus' Life

Jesus the Prophet

First, to provide some background, let us look at Jesus in his first-century Jewish context as an eschatological prophet. Eschatology just means 'of the end', at the end of all time, and restoration eschatology is the idea that at the end of time God will restore Israel. 'When will you restore the Kingdom to Israel, O Lord?' This is the great cry that goes up through the Hebrew Scriptures, the Psalms (Ps. 14.7, 53.6, 126.1) and the Prophets (Isa. 49.6; Jer. 29.14, 33.26; Ezek. 39.25), looking forward to God restoring the Kingdom to Israel in the end times.

Many prophets and teachers were around in the centuries before Jesus, and indeed during the first century. They would appear, often in the wilderness, some of them very wise and very holy men, others who were a bit mad and had perhaps spent too long in the sun, and they would come and gather a crowd together and say, 'Repent, the end of everything is at hand' — almost like some of the more wacky survivalist web sites today. There were a lot of such prophets and movements, and they were apocalyptic in nature (see boxes on pp. 15 and 24 above).

Jesus' Predecessor, John the Baptist

Chief among these prophets or wandering teachers was John the Baptist. John, like many others, spent a large amount of time in the desert. This was not just miles away from anywhere, but quite close to the edge of cities or farmland: the desert was where a lot of Jewish scholars and what we would perhaps call monks were living in communities. They went into the desert to get away from the pressures and the evils of the cities, and their legacy comes down to us in documents like the Dead Sea Scrolls. John may well have been influenced by these communities.

The Qumran Community

The Dead Sea Scrolls, discovered at Qumran near the Dead Sea, 1947-56, give us glimpses into the life of these desert communities, showing their concern for ritual washings before prayer, before meals and so on for purifying, as well as their beliefs about the coming Messiah. The community at Qumran probably consisted of Essenes who had withdrawn from more mainstream Judaism. The community was destroyed by the Romans in 68 CE.

John appeared preaching that people should repent, and the end of all things was at hand: the Kingdom of God was coming. As a sign of this, he suggested that people should be baptized. The word 'baptism' just means immersion under the water. If a non-Jewish man wanted to become a convert to Judaism, then he could be circumcised. A far more popular method — and open to women as well — was to become what was known as a God-fearer, a pious fellow-traveller, and the way to do this was to be baptized, as a way of washing away your impurity. What was different about John was that he was suggesting that even the people of God needed to be baptized.

Jesus was baptized by John. That is accepted as a historical fact by most people, because John preached the coming of somebody greater than himself. The early Christian movement had a problem about the fact that Jesus was baptized by John, because the superior should baptize the inferior. For Jesus to submit to baptism by John was actually a bit of an embarrassment to the early Church, and they had to explain it away. In one of the apocryphal Gospels, dating from the second century, Mary says, 'John the Baptist is baptizing everyone: let's pack up and go out for lunch and we can all get baptized.' And Jesus says to her, 'Why do I need to be baptized because I am sinless?' (*Gospel of the Nazarenes*, Fragment 2) This really sounds like a passage that has been made up to explain away something the writer found difficult, and the argument isn't very convincing. In the end, Jesus is baptized just to keep his mother happy.

But the fact that this text says something which is difficult to fit in is evidence that it probably happened. (cf. 'unintentionality', see p. 29). Moreover, even the canonical Gospels say that Jesus was baptized by John the Baptist, even though they then go on to show how Jesus is greater than John (e.g. Matt. 13-17; John 1.29-34, 3.22-30). Thus their apparent discomfort about it all suggests that this is what really happened.

Jesus' Followers

Like John the Baptist, then, Jesus set out on a ministry of what we call an itinerant preacher, wandering around. This was a typical habit of prophets and teachers of this period, gathering a group of followers. One of the remarkable things about Jesus' group was that it did include a significant number of women. For example, Luke 6.12-16 says that while Jesus had lots of followers, he chose out of them twelve men to be his inner circle. However, in chapters 8 and 10 we have references to the fact that Jesus accepted women as disciples, some of whom even helped to fund Jesus' work. Another story in Luke 10.38-42 tells us about Martha and Mary, two sisters. Mary sat at the feet of Jesus, listening to his teaching, and there was a protest from Martha who was out getting the dinner ready. She complains to Jesus about the fact that her sister has left her to do all the work, and Jesus says, 'No, this is important, Martha: Mary has chosen the better task. Sit down.' To 'sit at someone's feet' meant to become a disciple, so in saying this, he is accepting her as a disciple, and this acceptance of a woman is remarkable for that period. Again, this is not something that people would have invented, because it would have brought Jesus into disrepute: he would have been accused of having all sort of dubious friends — even treating women like men and accepting them as disciples at his feet!

Women as Jesus' Disciples

The twelve were with him, and also some women who had been healed of evil spirits and infirmities: Mary, called Magdalene, from whom seven demons had gone out, and Joanna, the wife of Chuza, Herod's steward, and Susanna, and many others, who provided for them out of their means (Luke 8.1b-3).

[Martha] had a sister called Mary, who sat at the Lord's feet and listened to his teaching (Luke 10.39).

So far we have established that Jesus was a prophet/teacher in the apocalyptic tradition, that he was baptized by John the Baptist, and that he had a group of followers which included women.

What Did Jesus Preach?

It is clear from all the texts that Jesus preached about the coming of the Kingdom of God (Matt. 4.23; Mark 1.15; Luke 4.43; John 18.36). The phrase 'Kingdom of God' is an unfortunate translation in many ways, because the word 'kingdom' is of course a political entity. Kingdoms have boundaries; they have kings, armies and customs posts and so on. The Hebrew word *malkuth,* and the Greek word *basileia,* actually mean the rule of God, the king*ship* of God, more than the king*dom* of God. It's not about a place, it's more about what happens when God's rule is recognized by people who actually put God as King, or Lord or Sovereign in their lives. This is quite different from many other Jewish teachers of the time who didn't just want the kingship of God, they wanted the kingdom of God — a free Israel, away from Roman oppression. Many of these would-be leaders were what we would now call 'freedom fighters', who were seeking the overthrow of the Romans (although no doubt the Romans would call them terrorists).

For Jesus to talk about the Kingdom of God was politically very dangerous. Among his followers we are told there were a couple who were described as 'zealots' (Luke 6.15; Acts 1.13; see box on p. 14 above). The Zealots were people with great 'zeal' — great enthusiasm — for Israel, and this was another term for revolutionaries, or freedom fighters.

Yet what Jesus says about the Kingdom of God is quite different from the political concept. He says it is 'near', 'at hand', 'among you' — you should respond to it (Luke 11.20). He says that his activity is bringing in the Kingdom. This became an issue when he was doing exorcisms. This was a way of healing people who were manifesting what was believed at the time to be spirit possession. Some people today have problems with that, although it's common in a lot of cultures even today as well as in the past. Jesus was clearly renowned as a great exorcist, among many exorcists at the time: the debate was not whether he could do it or not, but whose authority he was using (Mark 3.22). When he was commanding evil spirits was he using God's authority or the Devil's authority?

The same issue arose when he was healing people. There were many healers around at that time, and although this is something quite alien for some in our culture, others these days are moving back to a much more holistic sense of human beings as body, mind and spirit. The debate in Jesus' time was 'Whose authority, whose power is it he is using?' When he was doing these miracles, he said they were a sign that 'the Kingdom of God has come upon you'. His argument was that in all the prophetic books about the Kingdom of God (e.g., Isa. 61.1-2) it was written that the deaf would hear, the blind would see, the oppressed would be set free, the poor and the hungry would be fed. Now, in their own time, it was happening (Luke 4.14-21; 7.18-23).

Jesus talked a lot about the Kingdom of God, particularly to those who were outside, on the margins of society. His hallmark, as it were, was the combination of preaching and teaching with healing and accepting people, especially those outside the normal social and religious groups, as in his acceptance of women. Also, he spoke to Samaritans and even healed some of them. Some of the terrible problems we are now seeing in Israel-Palestine today go back to the roots of that argument between the Jews who went into exile and later came back to Jerusalem, and those Jews who stayed there in the area around the north of Jerusalem and became known as Samaritans. While Jews from Galilee would make a long detour down the Jordan river to reach Jerusalem without going through Samaritan villages, Jesus took a different approach. Against the conventions of his culture, Jesus accepted Samaritans — and even used one of them as the example of how to love your neighbour in the well-known parable of the Good Samaritan (Luke 10.25-37).

Samaritans: descendants of the Jews who continued living in Samaria — what we now call the West Bank of the river Jordan — after its fall to Assyria in 722-721 BC. They did not go into exile in Babylon in the sixth century BC and were despised for their mixed ancestry by the Jews who returned from exile.

Jesus even accepted Romans, the hated foreign rulers of the land (Luke 7.2-10). He accepted lepers who were social outcasts (Luke 5.12-16; 17.11-19). In the story in Mark 2.15-17 we read about his acceptance of those on the margins of society — and it was to them that he directed much of his preaching and teaching.

Most of his teaching was done in what we call parables, little stories. We can find a collection of Jesus' stories about the Kingdom of God in Matthew chapter 13.

- The Kingdom of God is like a sower going out to sow seed — and it grows, and that is what the kingdom is like (Matt. 13.3-23).
- The Kingdom of God is like a field full of weeds and wheat, where the weeds all grow alongside the plants and the flowers — and there comes a time when it is harvested, and the weeds are burned and the good fruit is used (Matt. 13.24-30).
- The Kingdom of God is like a seed growing secretly: you put it in the ground, and you come back and miraculously, there's a plant (Matt. 13.31, 32).
- The Kingdom of God is like yeast in a loaf that helps the loaf to grow and to rise (Matt. 13.33).
- The Kingdom of God is like treasure in a field. Someone has buried treasure and not come back for it, and you find it, and you have to sell everything to buy the field, without telling anyone that you have found treasure in it, so you can get the treasure (Matt. 13.44).
- The Kingdom of God is like a pearl of great price, and the merchant, who loves pearls, sells the rest of his pearl collection to raise the money to buy the one pearl (Matt. 13.45, 46).

So Jesus spent a lot of time saying what the Kingdom of God is *like*, although he never actually says what it *is*. But the core idea is that it is the activity of God, and that human beings have to respond to it, that you have to open your eyes, and see what God is doing. Above all, it's urgent: you have to enter the Kingdom, and if you don't do it now, the end is coming and there will be a settling of accounts (Matt. 7.13).

Another fact we learn about Jesus is that this teaching led to tremendous debate between Jesus and other groups within Judaism. Jews are passionate about interpreting the Law. Jonathan Sacks, the Chief Rabbi of Great Britain, is one of the visiting professors of King's College where I work, and he's fond of saying that wherever you've got two rabbis, you've got three opinions! They love nothing better than arguing and debating, because the Law is so important to them, and they have to work out what God is saying by arguing and debating it. So Jesus is engaged in this kind of debate with all the other interpreters of the Law, but there is growing opposition, partly because of his habit of 'opening up the Kingdom to the wicked' as they put it. Their attitude was, if you want to discover the Kingdom, fine: go to the temple, make sacrifice — but don't just give it away free, especially not to women and Samaritans and non-Jews in the way Jesus was doing.

Jesus' Death

This all came to a head when Jesus came to Jerusalem for Passover and held what we would now call a demonstration in the temple. We know from our TV screens, sadly, how crucial that bit of Jerusalem is today. Jesus goes to that area and is outraged by what is going on in the buying and selling in the courts, so he turns over the tables and creates a kind of demonstration (Mark 11.15-17). For many people that would have been the sign they were looking for, the moment when they were going to rise up, kill the Romans and bring in their own leaders.

Amazingly, Jesus doesn't do this at all. Instead, in Mark 11, there is an argument about 'What is his authority for doing it?' He is arrested, quizzed by the religious authorities and then taken to the Roman political authorities as a trouble-maker. When you've got hundreds of thousands of people crowded into Jerusalem, the last thing that either the religious or political authorities want is a trouble-maker, stirring up political unrest in the temple. So Jesus is executed on a charge of being 'The King of Jews' — or a claim to be the King of the Jews. The preaching about the Kingdom would be quite sufficient to condemn him.

Crucifixion of trouble-makers was a typical Roman response. Prophets like Jesus were two a penny in the first century. They come out of the wilderness, collect a few followers, or maybe quite a lot, they come to Jerusalem and make trouble. The best way to deal with the problem for the Romans was to execute the leader: the followers would always just disappear. We read in Acts 5.36-37 that this happened in the case of Theudas and Judas the Galilean.

What Happened Next?

In Jesus' case, they were up against something quite different, because the followers did not disappear. As we saw in the last chapter, without early Christian belief in the resurrection there would have been no Church. Whatever you believe about Jesus of Nazareth, you have to contend with the fact that a significant movement developed from the fact that his followers believed that he was risen from the dead. His disciples, just a bunch of frightened people at the crucifixion, were turning Jerusalem upside down just a few weeks later with their preaching and teaching about Jesus: many of them went on to die for him.

In the New Testament two things are said about the aftermath of Jesus' death. One is that the tomb was empty. Mark 16 tells us the women went to grieve, and found the tomb empty. Of course, graverobbers were emptying tombs all the time. The problem is that robbers would take the linen and the spices, because they had a commercial value, and leave the body. In the case of Jesus, it appears to have been the other way round. It's the body that has gone, and the linen and spices that are left.

The second phenomenon the New Testament describes is a long list of apparent appearances of the crucified Jesus, the first of which is to Mary Magdalene. In a Jewish court of the time, the word of a woman was not acceptable testimony. If the Christians wanted to claim that Jesus had appeared to somebody, they would not have chosen, as a first witness, somebody whose witness was not valid in court. So some people argue for the historicity of the resurrection in this way.

In 1 Corinthians 15.5-8, St Paul has a list of people to whom Jesus appeared. It's a very, very early list, much earlier than the Gospels, dating from only a few years after Jesus' death. He says, if Jesus wasn't raised from the dead then the Christians are deluded, and they are of all human beings most to be pitied. He goes on to say, 'Jesus appeared to Peter, to the twelve, to a group of five hundred, and to me', implying 'If you don't believe it, come and ask us.'

Many people have tried to explain these events in different ways — that it was fraud, that the disciples went to the wrong tomb, that there were hallucinations — and people argue back and forth. For me, a key fact that cannot be explained away is that in all the other groups, the death of the leader ended the movement. Here, quite to the contrary, the death of the leader was the beginning of something immensely greater.

Conclusion

So what facts have we considered to be historically valid about Jesus? First, Jesus of Nazareth existed, he was baptized by John the Baptist and gathered a controversial group of followers. He had an itinerant ministry preaching about the Kingdom of God. This led to opposition, and he was executed by Pontius Pilate.

It is no less a historical fact that after Jesus was dead and buried, an extraordinary event happened which transformed the once-terrified disciples and gave rise to a movement which we know as the early Church. From this initially fragile basis, Christianity spread through the rest of the world and through history and changed them for ever.

Jesus in the Gospels

At the beginning of the New Testament we have four books — Matthew, Mark, Luke and John, and they are known as 'Gospels'.

> **Gospel**: the Greek word for Gospel, *euangelion*, just means 'good news' and the word 'Godspell' in Anglo-Saxon is the same idea of 'good news' with good spelt with one 'o', which obviously brings in the idea of God as well. Good news is also used of an announcement and the Greek word *euangelion* was used for imperial proclamations — for news about an emperor or news of a victory.

What Are the Gospels?

From a literary point of view they are four short books, between ten and twenty thousand words in length, concentrating on the person of Jesus of Nazareth.

I am originally a classicist, teaching Latin and Greek before I was ordained, and I taught about types of literature such as epic, tragedy, comedy and so on. When I came to do my doctoral research, I found myself asking 'What kind of books are the Gospels?' This was later published as a book called *What Are the Gospels? A Comparison with Graeco-Roman Biography* (1992).

The Genre of the Gospels

To summarize briefly, the debates in this area focus on the word 'genre'.

> **Genre**: a French word that is used in English because there is no direct English equivalent; it means literary type or kind, pattern or family. Some people prefer to use the word *genus*, which is Latin, or *Gattung*, which is German.

Genre is a key convention in the interpretation of anything. If I say to you, 'Good evening, here is the news', I have already indicated to you the genre of what will follow. It will be a news broadcast, it will be about the latest events of the day in the Middle East, and what's going on in Westminster and Washington, and it will try to have equal air-time for both sides of the political debate — these are some of the expectations you have, because of the conventions of the genre. If I say, 'Once upon a time . . .' I tell you to expect a fairy story. It will be all about dragons and damsels in distress, and you won't worry too much if the dragon's side of the story doesn't get the same air-time as the damsel. We distinguish clearly between news and fairy story — that is unless you are watching cable TV or reading the tabloids! You need to know what it is you are listening to in order to interpret it. It is absolutely crucial that you interpret news broadcasts as though they are news broadcasts, fairy stories as though they are fairy stories and soap operas as though they are soap operas.

Genre is like a kind of contract between the author and the reader, or between the producers of a programme and the audience, about how they will write or produce something and how you should interpret what they have written. Therefore it is important that you should know what the genre of the thing is before you come to interpret it. Those who were brought up on the Arthur Ransome stories, *Swallows and Amazons,* will know that they are all about English middle-class kids who have nothing better to do in the summer in the 1930s than spend all their time sailing around on Windermere in the Lake District. They signal to each other with little flags. One thing you can do with flags is you can give a short wave or a long wave, and therefore you can use

Morse code. Or you can put the flags in different positions and you can do semaphore. The problems come, of course, if one person is signalling in Morse and you only know semaphore or vice versa. You have to know the code before you can interpret the message — and using the wrong code leads to problems.

Are the Gospels Biographies?

Traditionally, the Gospels were interpreted as stories about Jesus, particularly therefore as biography (Greek: *bio-graphe* — the writing of a life). The problem is that the word *biographe* only appears for the first time in the ninth century after Christ. Then during the nineteenth century, biography as a literary genre grew enormously, particularly after the understanding of human personality that came in through the work of Freud. There was a great attempt to look at what makes a person tick the way they do. Readers started asking, 'What is their personality?' They came to expect long stories about the subject's upbringing, their childhood, their schooling and so on. They wanted to see the character set in their life and times, an attempt to explain what their significance is in an international sense. So you can read about Winston Churchill's life and times, stories about his upbringing, where he went to school, and childhood intimations of being special, which is why he grew up believing in himself. You expect details of all the places in which he served in South Africa, and eventually a long discussion of the Second World War. This is what the genre of biography means to us today.

The more biography grew and developed, the less the Gospels looked like biography. They are very short. They don't tell us anything about Jesus' education or early years. They don't say he grew up thinking he was the Son of God because of childhood intimations, or any stories like that. They don't tell us much about the first thirty years or so of his life, they just go straight in at the period when he is baptized by John the Baptist and starts preaching. They don't tell us how old he was then, they don't give us a consistent time scale, and they don't put the narrative in any kind of context of the Roman empire. The Gospels came to look very different from what we know as biography today.

In the early part of the twentieth century, two writers, Rudolph Bultmann (who was mentioned in the last chapter in connection with

49

form criticism) and a colleague, Karl-Ludwig Schmidt, argued that the Gospels were a form of collection of folk tales, of stories that have been passed down through oral tradition. This means that we can't ask literary questions about who wrote them, or what kind of book they are, because the person who wrote them was just a kind of recording machine who wrote down the stories that came to them. Therefore they decided the Gospels are unique, they are *sui generis* — in Latin, 'of their own genre' or type. Whatever else they are, Bultmann said, they are not biographies, because they don't tell us all the things we would expect them to, and there is altogether too much focus on the death of Jesus.

The Contribution of Redaction Criticism

So really you couldn't even ask the question, 'What are the Gospels?' from the 1920s until the early 1980s. However, during the 1960s and 1970s came the development of redaction criticism which we looked at in Chapter 2. This is just the German word (since all this work was coming out of Germany) for newspaper editor. 'Redaction criticism' I translated as editorial criticism. This is the idea that if you look in the newspapers, even though they are all in the genre of newspaper, there are different sorts. You get used to the idea that the papers on one side of the political fence, like *The Wall Street Journal* or *The Daily Telegraph* report things in one way, and that on the other side *The Guardian* or *The New York Times* will have a different attitude, while the tabloids will sensationalize things. If they are reporting a speech by Margaret Thatcher, *The Telegraph* will be wildly in favour of the Conservatives, *The Independent* will be against them and *The Sun* will tell you what colour dress Lady Thatcher was wearing. In America the papers are often more concerned with a local slant, or a local issue which may be affected. You get used to the idea that although they are all newspapers, they have their own editorial policies. During the 1960s and 1970s there was a keen interest among theologians for doing detailed comparisons particularly of Matthew, Mark and Luke, saying, 'Why is it that Matthew always tells a story in this particular sort of way?' Because much of Mark reappears in Matthew and Luke, they were particularly interested in how the stories or the structure had been adapted in each case. In the jargon of today we could say, 'What's his spin on it?' What is his editorial interest? Why is that Luke, when he tells the same story, puts a different spin on it?

Once you accept that line of thought, you are beginning to see the Gospels as unified books. You can talk about their authors as people with particular interests, and therefore you can actually start asking questions again about what sort of books they are. That was the point at which I started my doctoral research and compared the Gospels with classical biography from the point of view of their generic features — their length, mode of representation, their units, the literary sources they used, the characterization that they used, their content, their aims and so on.

What was immediately apparent was that Bultmann was absolutely right to say that Gospels don't look anything like what *we* call biography. On the other hand, none of the ancient biographies (which they just called 'Lives' in the ancient world) look like anything we call biography either. What we call biography today is a product of the nineteenth century, and by definition the centuries around Jesus were not influenced by that. Actually, ancient Lives tend to be written in continuous prose narrative, between 10,000 and 20,000 words in length. It's what you can get on a single scroll. Remember they didn't have books: we're talking about a papyrus or a parchment scroll maybe thirty feet long. The idea of a scroll was that it was something that took about an hour and a half to read out loud. That was the primary method of publication. It would be read out loud after a dinner party or something as entertainment. These Lives were designed to be read at a single sitting, and so often they were confined to a bare chronological outline. The ancients weren't interested in personality and all the post-Freudian stuff, but they were interested in character, particularly moral character, and they wanted to hear about the understanding of the person in terms of their public life. Very often the text goes straight in at the point when the person becomes emperor, or for a writer, when they won a drama contest in Athens, or for a philosopher, when they first started their work. It will end at the death of the subject, and a huge amount of space will be given to the death because the ancients believed that how someone died was very significant for understanding their life. Death was seen as a climax to life, a way of summing up what a person really was. In between you have relevant material about their ideas on this or that subject. So both in terms of their structure and in terms of what they contain, the Gospels look very much like what we call ancient Lives, even though they don't look like what we call modern biography.

What Is the Subject of the Gospels?

When we talk in grammatical terms about the 'subject' of a sentence, we mean the identity of the person doing or saying something. If you add up all the grammatical subjects of each sentence in a longer text, you find the 'subject' of the book. I did this for the Gospels as a whole.

In ancient biography, if you do a structural analysis of the material, something like 25-30 per cent of the verbs of a biography have the hero as the subject, plus another large part which is given over to quotations from them — sayings, speeches and teaching and so on. We see exactly the same in the Gospels. Jesus is the subject of 25 per cent of the verbs in Mark and speaks a further 20 per cent of them. In Matthew and Luke he is the subject of 18 per cent of the verbs, and 40 per cent are Jesus speaking. So all of the Gospels, including John, have half of their verbs either with Jesus as either the subject, or on his lips. Only in ancient Lives do you find that kind of extraordinary concentration upon a person, with exactly the same emphasis in structural analysis of the subject of the verbs. This is because the Gospels are in the form of ancient Lives. They have this concentration on their understanding of the kind of person they are writing about.

The Gospels as a Form of Narrative Christology

> **Christology**: the study of Christ, or an understanding of 'Who is Jesus?'

The Gospels are not just a window through which we can look at the historical Jesus, nor are they a mirror in which we catch our own reflection. They are like a piece of stained glass. The point about that is the picture in the glass. The artist only has a limited amount of space. The kind of thing they will put in is limited, and everything you see through the window is coloured by the glass. So too, for Matthew, Mark, Luke and John. They have a limited amount of space — one scroll — and in each case they select things because they want to tell you something about their particular understanding of Jesus, what they want you to see. The Gospels are Christology in narrative form — the story of Jesus.

Four Portraits of Jesus

What difference does it make if we read the Gospels as though they were concentrating on Jesus, rather than as books that are just about the early Church's beliefs and theology? Does it help our understanding of the Gospels to interpret them as four attempts to give portraits of Jesus? In the title of my book, *Four Gospels, One Jesus?* (1994), the question mark is significant. If the Gospels are stories about Jesus, have we got four Gospels and four Jesuses, or could we have forty-four? Is there really one Jesus?

The Four Creatures

The prophet Ezekiel has a vision of the throne of God (Ezek. 1.10), where he sees living creatures around the throne with four faces — human, lion, ox, and eagle. These creatures appear again in the last book of the Bible (Rev. 4.7) where the same four creatures — the lion, ox, eagle, and human — are gathered around the throne of God. By the middle of the second century, the early Christians were very much into symbolic interpretation and wanted to know 'Who do these four creatures represent?' Since there were four, and their function was to tell us about Jesus, early Christians decided they stood for the four Gospel writers, so these four creatures got used as images of the Gospels. Particularly in a non-literate age, through the first centuries and especially the Celtic period in Britain, beautifully illuminated, wonderfully coloured manuscripts of the Gospels were created, such as the *Book of Kells* and the *Lindisfarne Gospels*. On the front of them would be a lion or an ox or an eagle along with wonderful Celtic art in the margins. So even if you can't read, you can see there's an eagle on the scroll, and you know this is the Gospel of St John.

Another use of these images is seen in St Mark's Square in Venice, which is surrounded by lions. I have also seen them all over the United States, from the dining hall and chapel of the General Theological Seminary, New York, to the lectern at the University of the South in Sewanee, Tennessee, and in stained glass from the Catholic Cathedral of Albany, capital of New York State, to churches in Vancouver, Canada.

When I was looking for a way to help people get a clearer picture of the four pictures of Jesus, I played with these images. Not that I think Jesus really is a lion, or an ox, but I wanted to explore what happens if we interpret Jesus in the light of Mark's picture of him with this overriding image of the lion, or Luke's picture of an ox. Many people read the Gospels as if they are interchangeable, but in fact each has its own perspective, its particular message and a distinctly different atmosphere. Let's bring these out by looking at each picture in turn.

Mark: The Roar of the Lion

Mark is the shortest Gospel, with only just over 11,000 words, and has some 665 verses. The Greek in which it is written is quite primitive, in the sense that it is simple Greek, written by somebody who clearly doesn't have Greek as his first language. In fact the writer is a native speaker of Aramaic, the popular form of Hebrew which was being spoken around the time of Jesus, and is still used by some Palestinians today. The verbal structure of Mark's language is very Aramaic, like Hebrew in many ways.

Mark's Pace

It's a very direct, vivid and immediate Gospel. When I applied the image of a lion to represent Mark, it was interesting to see how Jesus leaps onto the stage and bounds around. The text doesn't have any background to Jesus, how old he was, his ancestry or anything you might expect. It jumps straight in with an unexplained adult Jesus appearing (Mark 1.9). In the next verse we have the little phrase 'and immediately' when Jesus comes to be baptized by John the Baptist. In the first chapter of Mark alone this little phrase 'and immediately' comes ten times. This is an indication of the vividness and the pace which Mark puts into his picture of Jesus. He uses the phrase over forty times in his book, which is about the same number of times it appears in the rest of the New Testament put together. Mark obviously wants to inject some pace into his book.

Mark also likes to use what we know as the historic present. You may have heard a couple of old ladies talking about something that happened last week, or maybe fifty years ago, but they keep talking in the present. 'So I says to her, and she says to me'. It's as though the past event is so vivid to them that they talk about it in the present and the here and now. Mark does this all the way through his Gospel, trying to make it very present, very immediate. Everything is happening here and now. You won't find it so much in English translations because it is not good English style. The translators have tended to conclude that Mark needs correcting, and they have put it in the past tense for him. You have to read New Testament Greek, or read a very literal translation, to pick up this point.

Mark has sixteen chapters in three main sections, and the first section is chapters 1–8. This shows growing and developing conflict. Jesus appears on the public stage and rushes around, a bit like a roaring lion, teaching and healing and exercising a ministry of delivering people from evil. There is rising conflict, from his family — who think he is beside himself — from many of the other teachers who argue with him, and eventually with the religious and political authorities. Behind it all, says Mark, there is also the cosmic conflict with the powers of evil. All of those different conflicts are brought together in a story in Mark 3.19-35. We read there that Judas Iscariot is going to betray him, his friends think he is mad, the scribes decide he is possessed by demons, and he talks of his own ministry of exorcism in terms of conflict with cosmic powers of evil.

Jesus is obviously a teacher in Mark, because he is often called 'Rabbi', but there is not a lot of teaching and what we read is quite enigmatic so that even his disciples who have been with him all along keep getting the wrong end of the stick. Jesus gets quite exasperated with them: 'Don't you understand?' he sighs in 4.13, and 6.52 and 8.21 and again in 9.32.

There's been a lot of debate about why Mark shows the disciples as not understanding. Is this about the different groups or arguments within the early Church? Well, if we are looking at the narrative from the point of view of Mark's Christology, what is going on is that Mark is trying to say something about Jesus: that he is hard to understand, tough to follow, and if you don't get it right the first time, then don't be surprised because the disciples didn't either. If the great heroes like Peter can get it wrong, then there's hope for the rest of us yet. That's the image of Jesus that he's creating through the picture of his disciples not understanding.

Jesus' Identity

The first section of Mark introduces the furious pace of the lion rushing about roaring and fighting, but for the middle section we might change into musical terms, because we come into the slow movement (chapters 8–10). This section raises the question of identity. What kind of creature do we have here? Who is this person who makes such claims, who does such teaching, who can heal people, who can deliver people from evil? Through the middle chapters of Mark a number of answers are tried out. Jesus is an enigmatic wonder-worker. He heals people and yet he tells them not to tell anybody. He is the eschatological prophet, the prophet of the end times, but confusingly he says that the end times are coming now. He is the Messiah, but when he is recognized as Christ he tells Peter and the others not to tell people who he is. He is even hinted at as being the Son of God, but whenever he speaks of himself he prefers to use the phrase 'Son of man' — referring to himself in a slightly allusive way. He's going to Jerusalem, not actually to kick out the Romans and to bring in the Kingdom of God by military means, but to suffer and to be killed (8.31-32; 9.31-32; 10.33-34). When his disciples realize that, they say, 'No, that mustn't happen'. It is difficult for them, and us, to get our minds round such a contradictory, enigmatic figure.

When he comes to Jerusalem and the temple (Mark 11), it's like the lion returning to his lair, and yet the story is that he finds it a robbers' den. We read of the demonstration in the temple discussed in the last chapter. Jesus makes the accusation that the temple, which is supposed to be a place of prayer, has become a place for buying and selling (Mark 11.15-19).

This theme of something not being as it should be is very important in Mark. Jesus tells a parable about vineyards that don't produce their fruit when the master comes (Mark 12.1-11), and Jesus himself goes to the fig tree expecting to find figs but doesn't. All of these things — vineyards, fig trees and the temple — are used throughout the Hebrew Scriptures for the people of God. So when there are no grapes, no figs, no prayer in the temple, it's a warning: 'God is coming to his people: are you ready? If not, there will be destruction.' In Mark 13 Jesus warns in a prophecy that the temple will be destroyed, and this happened forty or so years later in 70 CE.

The Passion in Mark

In the final section, chapters 14 and 15, the active person stops rushing around and becomes very passive. He stops speaking, he is arrested, says nothing in his defence, suffers, and is executed as a criminal in dark desolation. His last words are 'My God, my God, why have you forsaken me?' (Mark 15.34). Even those words are misunderstood. At that precise moment, for the first time, a human being describes him as the Son of God. That human being is just a single Roman centurion at the foot of the cross.

Even the ending, in Mark 16, is full of enigma, and fear and awe. The manuscripts break off at the end of verse 8. There is an empty tomb, there are angels, the women go to the tomb and they are told that Jesus is alive and that they are to go and tell people — but they go out and because they are afraid, they say nothing. We are left wondering whether these disciples will still follow Jesus to Galilee and see him again.

It's a very interesting portrait of quite an enigmatic and problematic Jesus, who has a sense of being sent from God, and yet is constantly misunderstood.

Matthew's Human Face: The Teacher of Israel

Whereas Mark's image is this really rather frightening and difficult lion, Matthew is traditionally given the image of the human face, the teacher of Israel. The text of Matthew is quite a lot longer: it's over 18,000 words and over 1,000 verses.

Matthew's Sources

The content comes from three main sources. About half of Matthew is actually repeating Mark. He's clearly got a copy of the scroll of Mark open on the desk in front of him, and as he writes, he copies from Mark. We all know that plagiarism is a very bad thing these days, and if you copy others' work in exams you will be excluded. In the ancient world, on the contrary, it was a very good thing, because to copy someone else was to pay a compliment to their authority as one who has gone before you, and you put yourself under the authority of the one who had gone before. That's true of classical writers as it is of biblical writers. But at the same time, they felt perfectly at liberty to rewrite as they felt the need. Matthew corrects Mark's Greek where it is too Aramaic, and explains and contracts or expands Mark as he goes. So half of Matthew comes from Mark, and the other half is divided into quarters: one comes from a shared source that Matthew has with Luke. (See Figure 1 on p. 27.) This document, which is postulated but which we don't have, is known to theologians as Q, from *Quelle*, which is the German word for 'source'. It was probably a list of the teachings of Jesus. Critics have made much use of Q, although we don't actually have that document. (If you follow *Star Trek: The Next Generation*, you will know that Q is a figure that can appear and disappear and take any form he likes: I enjoy pulling the legs of New Testament scholars by suggesting that their use of Q is not dissimilar.)

A Jewish Teacher

Matthew is very keen to show this human face, this teacher of Israel. The spin that he puts on the story all the way through is that he is clearly writing for a Jewish audience. He keeps showing how everything that happens is fulfilment of ancient prophecy. You have to know your Hebrew Scriptures very well to actually appreciate what he is on about a lot of the time.

Old Testament Prophecy in Matthew

There is a recapitulation of the Moses story to suggest that Jesus is another Moses, the Liberator, to teach Israel again that 'God is salvation'.

- The infant is saved from an evil king intent on slaughtering babies (Exod. 1.15–2.10 and Matt. 2.16-18).

- He has to flee for his life and grow up in another land (Exod. 2.15-22 and Matt. 2.13, 14).

- He returns only after the death of the king (Exod. 2.23 and Matt. 2.19-20).

- This involves taking wife and son (Exod. 4.20 and Matt. 2.21).

Jesus, as the Teacher of Israel, is depicted as another Moses.

- Israel in Egypt is described by God as 'my firstborn son' (Exod. 4.22); Jesus is declared 'my Son' at his baptism (Matt. 3.17).

- The people of Israel were tested in the wilderness for forty years (Deut. 8.2); Jesus was tested for forty days and nights (Matt. 4.1-2).

- Moses went up onto the mountain to receive the teaching of God (Exod. 19.20) and afterwards came down to the people (Exod. 19.24-25); Jesus goes up onto a mountain to give his teaching to Israel (Matt. 5.1) and afterwards comes down to the people (Matt. 8.1).

- Moses is shown the land of Israel from a mountain (Deut. 34.1-4), while Jesus sees 'all the kingdoms of the world' (Matt. 4.8).

So Matthew talks about Jesus' Jewish background: he gives Jesus a genealogy that traces Jesus' descent through Joseph right back to the great heroes like David and on indeed all the way back to Abraham. There's a great stress on seeing things from the male point of view, so that the birth narratives are seen through Joseph's eyes. Jesus is portrayed as another Moses. He teaches from mountains just in the way Moses did. He doesn't get rid of the Jewish Law: far from it — he is fulfilling the Law and the Prophets (Matt. 5.17-20). Another Jewish 'message' is that Matthew collects together Jesus' teaching, particularly the Q material — the material he shares with Luke — into five great blocks — five sermons, five speeches. The first one, chapters 5–7, is best known as the Sermon on the Mount (another mountain as when Moses gave his teaching). These five sermons or speeches echo the first five books of the Bible, the Torah, or Hebrew Scriptures. What Matthew seems to be saying is that Jesus is like Moses in having five blocks of teaching.

Only in Matthew do we have Jesus saying that his mission is to the lost sheep of the house of Israel (10.5-6). He repeats this when a Gentile woman comes up and wants some help (15.24). She presses him, and then because of her faith, he helps her as well.

Throughout Matthew's story we see the conflict between Jesus, who is the fulfilment of all the Jewish hopes, and the religious authorities of his own day who nevertheless oppose him. As they do so, Jesus starts to form a new community. Predominantly to begin with they are Jewish believers who believe he is the Messiah. The fourth block (chapter 18) is a block of teaching about the Church, and the fifth block consists of teaching about the end times (chapters 24–25) preceded by woes to the leaders of his own day (chapter 23).

The Passion in Matthew

In Matthew's account of Jesus' passion — his suffering and death — he has quite a debate about Judas who betrayed him, and the way in which Pilate washes his hands of Jesus. Rejection and conflict come from all around. And yet Jesus is clearly fulfilling prophecy. When we come to Jesus' cry of abandonment on the cross, which in Mark 15.34 is just a desolate cry, Matthew (27.45-54) describes not just darkness but an earthquake, the ground being shaken and the rocks splitting open, which is exactly the kind of thing that happens time and time again throughout the Hebrew Scriptures whenever God appears and intervenes in human experience. Matthew is saying, 'In that moment of utter desolation, as Jesus experienced acute human alienation, sin and lostness, yes even death, that was actually the ultimate revelation of God. God loves us so much that he comes to live among us in that way.'

Afterwards we have another earthquake at the tomb (28.2-4), Jesus meets the women (28.9) and the first witnesses, and there is a division in Israel between the soldiers who are telling lies and taking bribes and the disciples who are then told to go to the ends of the earth (28.16-20). We can infer from this that Matthew is probably writing around the time of the separation of church and synagogue after the Jewish War in the 80s — a very painful and bitter time. It's a book written predominantly for Jewish Christians who believe that Jesus is the Messiah, to help them to understand why they were thrown out of the synagogue and why Israel rejected their Messiah. Like all internal arguments, this separation is very bitter and Matthew read outside of that context will appear to some people to be very anti-Jewish, until you remember that it is written by someone who was Jewish himself. The Dead Sea Scrolls, and what they say about the Jewish leadership of the first century, are even more critical. But nobody describes the Dead Sea Scrolls as being anti-Semitic — you can't, because they are part of the internal debate of the day. Only Jewish comedians (and rabbis) are allowed to tell Jewish jokes! Matthew is the same. He is trying to do two things at once. He is trying to tell the basic story about Jesus, but he also trying to answer the question, 'Why did Israel reject him?' and to do that for Jewish Christian believers.

Luke's Burden-Bearing Ox

Luke, however, takes the same story and is writing for a completely different group. Whereas Matthew's Gospel is written for a very Jewish context, Luke writes for a very Greek or Roman, universal context. Matthew traces Jesus' descent back to Abraham, but Luke gives us a genealogy at the start that goes all the way back to Adam ('son of Adam, son of God' — Luke 3.38). It's the longest Gospel, over 19,000 words, some 1,149 verses, and he too uses Mark, but tends to weave together his sources. It's much more difficult to see blocks of material in the same way.

Table 1. Sources of material in Luke

Luke	Mark as source	Q and L material
1.1–3.2		is unique = L
3.3–4.30	mixes Mark 1.1-20	with Q and L
4.31–6.19	follows basically Mark 1.21–3.19	
6.20–8.3		combines Q and L
8.4–9.50	follows basically Mark 4.1–9.40	
9.51–18.14		combines Q and L
18.15–24.12	Mark 10.13–16.8	with L material
	inserted through Passion	
24.12-50		is unique = L

Table 1 shows how Luke mixes together Mark's material, the Q material he shares with Matthew, his own material (L), and large passages where he weaves it all together. Whereas Matthew sees the story from Joseph's point of view, Luke sees it from Mary's point of view. Jesus is seen among the women — Mary, Elizabeth — and also among the lowly poor. In Matthew's account it is the rich wise men from the East who come to see the baby Jesus, whereas in Luke it is the poor, humble shepherds (Luke 2.10-20). The animal representing Luke has always been the burden-bearing ox. Whereas Mark's opening passages have Jesus bounding around immediately as a rushing lion, Luke sets Jesus in a historical and geographical perspective, writing what he describes as an 'orderly account' (1.3) making steady progress like a plodding ox.

The Gospel is carefully structured historically. The opening chapters have a deliberate Old Testament feel, evoked by phrases common in the Hebrew Scriptures such as 'the house of', 'before the face of' and 'it came to pass'. This changes as Jesus and the disciples travel to Jerusalem, and the second volume of Luke's book, known as the Acts of the Apostles, takes them out into the whole Greco-Roman world.

Luke's Gospel divides into three main sections again with a geographical dimension. The ministry in Galilee takes up the first nine chapters, the middle section (chapters 9–19) moves down the Jordan valley towards Jericho, heading for Jerusalem. The final section, from chapter 19 to the end, is in Jerusalem itself.

Luke's Special Concerns

Luke is very keen to show Jesus' human development, and yet he is the one who calls him Saviour and Lord all the way through. Throughout the first part of Jesus' ministry, Luke constantly raises questions about Jesus' identity. Worshippers wonder in the synagogues of Nazareth (4.22) and Capernaum (4.36); questions are asked by the scribes and Pharisees (5.21), John the Baptist (7.19), the disciples (8.25) and Herod (9.9). Luke's first answer is to see Jesus as a prophet. The baptism scene reminds us of a prophetic anointing, with its stress on the descent of the Holy Spirit and the voice addressed to Jesus, 'You are my beloved Son'. There are references to Elijah and Elisha in 4.16-30, and the raising of the widow's son recalls Elijah's similar miracle (Luke 7.11-17 compared with 1 Kings 17.17-24). It seems from 7.16, 9.8 and 9.19 that the crowds saw him as a prophet, and Jesus compares himself with Jonah (11.29-32), talks about the rejection and murder of prophets in 11.47-52 and makes a prophetic journey to the holy city because 'it cannot be that a prophet should perish away from Jerusalem' (13.33).

The disciples are a much wider group than just the twelve. Luke talks about how much the crowds followed Jesus, and particularly tells us about women disciples (Luke 8.1-3; 10.38-42). He talks about another group called the seventy (10.1-6), and about the enthusiastic crowds. The disciples understand what is going on a lot better in Luke's account, and the Pharisees who seem to have those bitter arguments in Matthew, here spend a lot of time inviting him to dinner where they have a lot of religious debate. The real opposition comes from the chief priests, the Sadducees, the spiritual leaders who control the temple at Jerusalem and know how to execute an ox that doesn't stay in its place.

Throughout Luke's Gospel, Jesus is concerned for the poor, the lost, the unacceptable, the outcast, women, Gentiles and so on. That's why the image of the ox, the burden-bearer, is a very appropriate one. He is sustained in his work by prayer (a theme which is underlined in this Gospel), and he is the one who gives the Holy Spirit. Luke refers to the Spirit eighteen times in his Gospel, and a staggering fifty-seven times in Acts, compared with six references in Mark and twelve in Matthew. The Holy Spirit initiates each stage of the Gospel, coming upon Mary, Elizabeth, Zechariah, John and Simeon between 1.34 and 2.27. At the start of the ministry the Spirit descends 'in bodily form' at Jesus' baptism and leads him both into (4.1) and out of (4.14) the wilderness. His manifesto at Nazareth in 4.18 begins with 'the spirit of the Lord is upon me', and there is another cluster of references as he sets his face towards Jerusalem (10.21; 11.13; 12.10, 12). Jesus is not only supremely the man of the Spirit, but is also the one who baptizes in the Holy Spirit (3.16), and where Matthew says that God will give his children 'good gifts' in Matthew 7.11, Luke's parallel passage says that the heavenly Father will give 'the Holy Spirit to those who ask him' (11.13). This promise is renewed by the risen Jesus (24.49) and fulfilled throughout the Acts of the Apostles.

The Passion in Luke

When we come to the story of the crucifixion in Luke, we find that Jesus dies as he lived. His farewell discourse to his friends provides for their continuing life with the Eucharist (22.15-20), warns them of betrayal (22.21-23), settles their dispute about their behaviour when he is gone (22.24-30) and establishes Peter as his successor to strengthen the others (22.31-34). He is concerned on the way to the cross for the women of Jerusalem, the women who are weeping for him, and he warns them of the coming destruction of Jerusalem (23.27-31). He prays for forgiveness — 'Father, forgive them, for they do not know what they are doing' — and for the humble soldiers who are executing him (23.34). And whereas for Matthew and Mark both the thieves on either side being crucified with him insult him, in Luke he says to the one thief who is penitent, 'Today you will be with me in paradise' (23.43). He dies not in desolate abandonment as in Matthew ('My God, my God, why have you forsaken me?') or being misunderstood as in Mark, but he dies as a man of prayer, still trusting God, like a child saying the Jewish night psalm, 'Father, into your hands I commend my spirit' (23.46).

Then after the resurrection, he reappears to his friends, he dines with them (24.43), and then Luke reminds us of his interest in history and geography as we are told the way in which the Christian message will go out from Jerusalem to the ends of the earth.

John's High-Flying Eagle

In length, John is in between Mark on the one hand and Matthew and Luke on the other. He has some 878 verses, about 15,500 words. In the Old Testament, eagles are used as an image of God's awesome, all-seeing, all-knowing ability, of God's tender care, where he bears people up on eagle's wings (Exod. 19.4), but also of his judgement, where he swoops down on the flock and carries off an animal (Jer. 48.40-41). All those things are true of John's portrait of Jesus.

John is quite different from the Synoptic Gospels. He shares the basic story of Jesus' ministry leading to conflict with the authorities and his subsequent passion, and some sayings, stories and events are similar to those in the Synoptic Gospels. However, he writes in a different style, with his own themes and vocabulary and with a different chronology — for example, the temple incident happens at the beginning in John 2, not at the end as in Mark 11. There are no parables or exorcisms. Jesus talks in extended discourses about himself rather than pithy sayings about the Kingdom of God. Many well-loved characters and incidents appear only in John — the wedding at Cana (2.1-11), Nicodemus (3.1-21), the Samaritan woman (4.1-42) and Lazarus (11.1-44).

The Divine Perspective

While Mark goes straight in with the baptism, while Matthew begins with the birth of Jesus, while Luke begins with the birth of John the Baptist who prepares the way for Jesus, John begins in John 1.1-18 with the really long-term picture. 'In the beginning was the Word, and the Word was with God, and the Word was God.' Jesus was actually pre-existent with God, was involved in the creation right at the start, and came from those incredible heights of divinity to take human form to live among us.

John structures his story in two main halves — the ministry for the first half (chapters 1–12), and the death and resurrection for the second half (chapters 13–21). Throughout them, Jesus is centre stage. He mixes together signs and discourse, activity and teaching. So we have for instance in chapter 6 the story of feeding a large multitude, and then a debate about the claim that Jesus is the true bread. In chapter 9 we have a story about the healing of a blind man, and a long discourse about the statement that Jesus is the light of the world. We have the raising of the dead, and the statement that Jesus is the resurrection and the life (chapter 11).

The easy style and repetitive vocabulary give this Gospel a surface simplicity: the meditative reflection undergirds it all with hidden depths. Conversations begin between Jesus and others about very human and natural things, like birth (3.3), water (4.7), bread (6.25ff.), or sight (9.1), but incomprehension and questions soon follow. Nicodemus cannot re-enter his mother's womb, the woman notices that Jesus has no bucket to get his water, the crowd want real bread to eat. Jesus invites them to see through to the 'spiritual realities' these 'earthly things' represent (3.12), while at a deeper level still the author delivers the same invitation to the reader.

John's picture begins with the high-flying perspective of the Prologue, but throughout the narrative Jesus never loses this knowledge: he is aware of his own pre-existence with God (6.38, 62; 17.5); he knows who sent him into the world and why he was sent (6.39), when his hour has not yet come (2.4) and when it does arrive (12.23; 13.1; 17.1), where he has come from and where he is going (7.33; 8.14, 21; 13.3), how he will get there (12.32-33) and the eventual destiny of all his people to be with him in his Father's glory which he had at the beginning (17.5, 24; 20.17).

However, despite his divine knowledge, John's Jesus gets weary and thirsty (4.6-7) and weeps at the death of a friend (11.35), snorting with rage at what has happened (11.33, 38). There is a tension between the divine and the human.

The Passion in John

There is a lot more theology, a lot more reflection about Jesus, in the way in which John says that Jesus is equal with the Father (10.30) and yet dependent on him. Throughout the story there is growing opposition from this group which John calls 'the Jews' — although you have to bear in mind that John was Jewish, Jesus was Jewish and the disciples were all Jewish. By this phrase, John means the Jewish leaders.

Lastly, Jesus spends his time with the disciples at the end (chapters 13–17), and even in the passion, he is in control, directing events. He chooses to lay down his life of his own volition (10.18), and explains it all to his disciples in a farewell discourse (14–17). He carries his own cross 'by himself' with no mention of Simon of Cyrene: his suffering is not stressed, but from the cross he is concerned about who is going to look after his mother, and he entrusts his mother to a friend of his, a disciple (19.26-27). He is still fulfilling Scripture, saying that he is thirsty, and he dies, not with a cry of desolation as in Mark and Matthew, or a cry of commitment as in Luke, but with a cry of triumph — 'It is accomplished' (19.30). Then we have the story of the resurrection in chapters 20 and 21 where he reappears to comfort Mary, challenge Thomas and restore Peter. In each case they are challenged to a new level of seeing, and this leads to a recognition of Jesus' identity as Lord. For the reader who has taken the higher perspective, this truth has been known from the start. The Word who was God in the beginning is now acknowledged as God at the end.

From Four Gospels Back to One Jesus

Now that we have seen the distinctiveness of each Gospel, we are faced with the question, what continuity is there between Jesus himself and the portraits? Do we talk of *Mark's Jesus,* implying that this is his own creation — or of *Mark's view of Jesus,* implying roots in a historical person whom the evangelist has appreciated in a particular way? Do the Gospel writers select appropriate material from their sources, or create it themselves? What is the relation between 'his story' and 'history' — and can 'his story' be true if it is not 'history'?

Unfortunately, some modern studies assume that if there is 'fiction' in the Gospels, then they are inauthentic or unreliable. However, closer attention to literary criticism shows that no one wrote a classical biography to provide a documented historical text as we might capture something with a tape recorder, but rather in an attempt to get 'inside' the person. Thus, John's stress on 'truth' is not about documented fact but the higher truth of who Jesus is, which is why he writes in a biographical format. For him, Jesus is 'the way, the truth and the life', so his Jesus says these words (John 14.6). To ask whether Jesus actually ever spoke those words is to miss the point completely. This is neither a lie nor fiction; it is simply a way of bringing out the truth about the subject which the author wishes to tell the audience.

Each gospel writer portrays his belief about Christ in his own distinctive way. In Mark, Jesus' identity is revealed through supernatural means, the demons and the heavenly voice, and is confirmed finally by the centurion at the cross: 'Truly this was the Son of God' (Mark 15.39). In Matthew we see Jesus being worshipped as God by the wise men at his birth, through the disciples in the storm-tossed boat, to the new community on the mountain. Luke makes the remarkable shift from using the phrase 'the Lord' to mean 'the Lord God' in the early chapters to making it his main term for Jesus: what God is, Jesus is. John makes this explicit, from the Prologue — 'the Word was God' right through to Thomas' confession — 'My Lord and my God'.

All four agree that in his deeds and words Jesus acts and speaks for God. He is not just a prophet, nor even the human agent of the Kingdom of God, for the extraordinary response is that of worship, worship which may only be given properly to God himself. There may be four Gospels, but there is only one Jesus, and he is God, come among us in human form.

Jesus and Paul

It is important to remember that the four portraits we explored in the last chapter were written at least a generation after Jesus died. Mark, the earliest, may have been put together by the mid-sixties — thirty years or so after Jesus — and the others during the seventies, eighties or even the nineties. When we turn to the person of Paul, we are moving a lot closer in time to Jesus himself. One of Paul's letters may well have been written within fifteen years of Jesus' death.

Interestingly, Paul actually tells us very little about the historical Jesus. You might expect such earlier material to tell you about the life of Jesus, and that later material would grapple with people's ideas and beliefs and theology. Some people have formulated an evolutionary view of the development of Christology, which suggests that as time went by, the followers' understanding of Jesus increased, and that he was more and more seen as divine. However, it is not as simple as that.

In the last chapter we saw that the Gospels, which are written later, are actually the ones that tell you about the life of Jesus. Of course, they have theology and understanding in them as well. What is significant about the Gospels is that the basic story that they tell is the same: they cover Jesus' appearance onto the public scene, and they spend about half of the time talking about his ministry of teaching, healing, preaching and fighting evil. The second half deals with the events of his arrest, trial and death and finally the resurrection — the empty tomb, the appearances and what happened next.

Even though they are free to write their own interpretation of Jesus, the actual sense of agreement among the four Gospels is very significant. So already it's a warning that early material does not necessarily mean historical, and later material does not necessarily mean theological, but actually it is a combination of the two going on throughout the first century.

From Jesus to Paul: Early Christian and Pre-Pauline Christology

When we move a generation back into the time of Paul, what is extraordinary is that Paul actually says very little about the earthly life and ministry of Jesus, and is much more interested in the theological impact and significance of that life. Paul wrote some of the earliest parts of the New Testament, but is there any way we can go back earlier still, to look at the period of about fifteen years between the death of Jesus and the first letter of Paul? Obviously, the theological, religious and spiritual assessment of Jesus at this period is absolutely crucial.

Of course, we don't have any documents before Paul's letters. But what we discover is that in Paul's letters there appear to be phrases, and even passages, which are in a slightly different style, or in some cases, use different vocabulary. In passages where Paul appears to be quoting earlier material, he puts us in touch with the pre-Pauline period, the period between Jesus and Paul.

In a number of places, Paul uses the technical word for 'handing on' the tradition, 'I handed on to you what was handed on to me'. Passages introduced by such a phrase, or when Paul seems to be quoting very early songs about Jesus, give us glimpses into an earlier world.

One thing that is clear about this very early period, the first decade or so after the life of Jesus, is that Jesus is already being worshipped. This is remarkable, of course, because Jesus was Jewish, the disciples were Jewish, and the early Christians were Jewish — strict monotheists, to whom the first commandment was 'You shall worship the Lord your God alone and nobody else.' How can it be that Jews of this period would actually take the extraordinary step, not just of worshipping an idol, or an emperor, or a personification, but actually somebody who they claimed was a human being, and had lived and died — and died shamefully — only a matter of a few years before? Something

---

Examples of 'Handing On' Passages

1 Corinthians 11.23: 'I received from the Lord what I also passed on to you: on the night that he was betrayed . . .'

1 Corinthians 15.3: 'What I have received I passed on to you as of first importance . . .'

1 Corinthians 11.10: 'I praise you for holding to the teachings just as I passed them to you.'

(See also 2 Thess. 2.15 and 3.6 for traditions handed on.)

---

very significant had clearly happened. We can obviously debate the historicity of the resurrection, and the evidence for it, but what is an absolutely incontrovertible fact is that it was the belief of the early Christians in the resurrection that brought about that startling change (see Chapter 1).

Jesus as the Wisdom of God

What we see, in the earliest level of material in the New Testament, is creative use being made of the Scriptures of the Hebrew people, as the first Christians tried to reflect on what Jesus was all about, and to understand the significance of what had happened. As Jews, they looked back to their Scriptures, and searched through all the prophecies, the passages throughout the Law, Prophets and Writings — what Christians now call the Old Testament.

In particular they found there a lot of Jewish traditions about the Wisdom of God. Through the Hebrew Scriptures there develops this idea of God's Wisdom as almost a separate person from God. It could be quite dangerous to put it as blankly as that, but perhaps it's safer to describe it as the personification of the Wisdom of God. Particularly in the Wisdom literature — the book of Proverbs, the book of Job, and the books that were written between the times of the two Testaments — this figure of Wisdom grows and develops. She — for it's a female figure

— often speaks in the first person and says 'I was with God in the beginning, I was involved in the creation, the Lord created me first, the Lord sent me to dwell among human beings and to teach them the Wisdom of God.' There is this idea that you can almost envisage the Wisdom of the one God as a personification, as a character who was involved in creation, in sustaining the world, but who also comes down to human level and teaches people about God and invites people to choose whether to respond to her or not.

Bible Passages about Wisdom

Wisdom is given by God to people — 1 Kings 3.28; Ezra 7.25

Search for Wisdom — Proverbs 2.1-15, 7.4

The figure of Wisdom — Proverbs 3.13-20, 8.1-36, 9.1-6; Job 28.12-28; Wisdom of Solomon 6.12-25, 7.21–8.9

Although this figure is described as distinct from God, it is absolutely clear that she is a personification of Wisdom, rather than in any sense being a second God. What the Jewish people were always very clear about was that God was the Lord, was One. The respect for God was so great that you would never say the name of God. When you read the Scriptures you just said, 'the Lord, *Adonai*' when the name of God was in the text. One of the first ways in which the early Christians seem to have interpreted the person of Jesus was in the light of those traditions about Wisdom, as a person who came from God and lived among human beings to teach them and bring them to God.

'Jesus Is Lord'

Secondly we find, very early on, clear evidence that the early Christians are calling Jesus 'Lord'. We know this because we read a very simple little prayer in Aramaic. When Paul is writing his letters to mixed congregations of Greek-speaking Jews and Greek-speaking Gentiles, it is interesting that he sometimes uses little words in Aramaic. One such example is the little prayer, 'Maranatha'. This is Aramaic for 'Our Lord, come', or 'O Lord, come'. The word *Mar* means Lord. We find this prayer throughout the Hebrew Scriptures; the prayer for the day of the Lord to come, the prayer for the end of all things: 'Come, O Lord, judge the earth, set your people free', begins with this phrase. What is extraordinary is that the early Christians took that prayer, 'Lord, come', and addressed it to Jesus. For example in 1 Corinthians 16.22-24 Paul says, 'Our Lord come. The grace of the Lord Jesus be with you. My love be with you all in Christ Jesus.' He's signing off. While the rest of the sentence is in Greek, 'our Lord come' is the Aramaic word 'Maranatha'. This prayer is picked up again in the last verses of the New Testament, in the book of Revelation (22.20-21) as 'Come, Lord Jesus.'

> **Aramaic** was the language of Jesus. It is the popular form of Hebrew which would have been spoken as the native tongue of people living around Galilee, Judaea and Jerusalem. A form of it still survives today, spoken by a small group in the area.

So in the use of this word, in the language of Jesus and the first disciples, long before the disciples were working in the Greek world, we already see that the Aramaic word *Mar* is being applied to Jesus of Nazareth. This term, usually reserved for God, then becomes frequent in its Greek translation, *kurios*.

This calling of Jesus 'Lord' means that monotheistic Jews were using a word which could only be used of God, and applying it to Jesus. This is an indication of how very soon the early Christians were treating Jesus as God. First Corinthians 12.3 underlines this. Paul is trying to deal here with the issue of people who would shout out in the fairly lively services they were having, and how you could know whether they were being inspired by God or by an evil spirit. And here he quotes, as it were, the first creed. 'If someone says, "Let Jesus be cursed", that is an evil spirit, and if they say, "Jesus is Lord", that is from God.' This is using the same idea, that of confessing Jesus as Lord. In Romans 10.9 he says that people who confess with their lips that Jesus is Lord are the ones who will be saved.

Early Credal Fragments

The other bit of pre-Pauline material to which I want to draw your attention is what we call early 'hymns', or credal fragments — a fragment of belief. As we saw in the first chapter, one of the strongest features that makes Christianity different from other religions, particularly its distinction within the monotheism of Islam and Judaism, is this pre-occupation with doctrine, rather than practice. Even in the early stages, expressions of creed, of belief, were being used.

In Paul's letters there are a number of 'mini-hymns'. These are passages where Paul, who is writing in prose, suddenly seems to lapse into something which has a poetic rhythm about it. Very often these little pieces include vocabulary which is not particularly Pauline. They are marked off from the rest of the text, and the assumption is that Paul is quoting a song, or a hymn, or a psalm, or a short expression of faith, which was used in early Christian worship, and which his readers will know, to prove his point.

Now, if this assumption is correct, it is evidence of pre-Pauline material. The best example is Philippians 2.6-11. In this letter to the Philippians, Paul is saying that they should respect one another and have unity and love one another — he is not actually trying to teach them about Jesus at the time. Then he says 'You should have this same mind among you which is yours in Christ Jesus, who . . .' and then he goes off into a more poetic style, which in some translations is marked out as poetry.

Now there is great debate about how much of that is pre-Pauline and how much is Paul, but it is very clear that Jesus is Lord to the glory of God. This passage has been used a great deal in church liturgies in the last two millennia. But it is indicative that the early Christians believed that the person of Jesus existed before the human being of Jesus of Nazareth. He was found in divine form, but emptied himself, taking the form of a slave, a human form, even died, and God has now exalted him as Lord. It is descending from God to become human, to live and to die, and then reascending back to God. This kind of pattern, descending and then going up again — like a 'v' or a 'u' — is echoed in other parts of the Bible.

We find an equally powerful Christology in another hymn that is often considered also to be a fragment preserved from pre-Pauline ma-

---

The Christ-Hymn in Philippians

Let the same mind be in you that was in Christ Jesus,
who, though he was in the form of God,
did not regard equality with God
as something to be exploited,
but emptied himself,
taking the form of a slave,
being born in human likeness.
And being found in human form,
he humbled himself
and became obedient to the point of death —
even death on a cross.
Therefore God also highly exalted him
and gave him the name
that is above every name,
so that at the name of Jesus
every knee should bend,
in heaven and on earth and under the earth,
and every tongue should confess
that Jesus Christ is Lord,
to the glory of God the Father.

(Philippians 2.6-11)

---

terial, in Colossians chapter 1. Again, Paul is not particularly trying to teach about the person of Jesus at the time. Here he's telling people to give thanks to God in Christ, and suddenly his thoughts are triggered off into a memory of this hymn or credal material.

Here we see Paul again drawing upon this figure of Wisdom, with the idea that, like Wisdom, Jesus was involved with God in creation, came among human beings, died, and that death was significant, and then he was exalted back to God.

So between the life of Jesus and Paul's writings, we have a very early expression of faith. It's not worked out in any kind of philosophical, theological or ontological fashion, but it is an expression of the ex-

The Christ-Hymn in Colossians

He is the image of the invisible God,
the firstborn of all creation;
for in him all things in heaven and on earth were created,
things visible and invisible,
whether thrones or dominions or rulers or powers —
all things have been created through him and for him.
He himself is before all things,
and in him all things hold together.
He is the head of the body, the church;
he is the beginning, the firstborn from the dead,
so that he might come to have first place in everything.
For in him all the fullness of God was pleased to dwell,
and through him God was pleased
to reconcile to himself all things,
whether on earth or in heaven,
by making peace through the blood of his cross.

(Colossians 1.15-20)

perience of the worship of the early Christians. They found that in the human life of Jesus of Nazareth and his teaching, the God of their Fathers, the God of Abraham, Isaac and Jacob, was being made known to them, just as their Scriptures described the Wisdom of God. Their experience was also that after his death, that same person was being made known to them in their worship, through what they then came to call the Spirit of God, and that they were worshipping him not only as the risen Christ, but as the Christ who existed before he was born, who came and lived among human beings and has now returned to be with God, where he can be worshipped as 'Lord'.

Paul

Outline of Paul's Life

Paul does not actually write a huge amount about himself in his letters, for the obvious reason that he is writing about his belief about Christ. We don't know when he was born, but he seems to be the same sort of age as Jesus or perhaps a little younger. By the mid-thirties, which is the first time we hear about him, he is already very active, clearly theologically trained, and has been involved in a lot of activities, so he's probably at least thirty, or perhaps in his late twenties. That means he was probably born about the year zero, or in the first few years of the first century, in Tarsus, in Asia Minor. He came from a strict Jewish family, but his father was also a Roman citizen. Paul worked, all his life — when he wasn't doing his 'religious' work — as a manufacturer of tents. It is possible that he inherited the family business, that his father could have been a maker of tents for the occupying Roman army in Asia Minor in the campaigns of that period, and that could be why his father was honoured with Roman citizenship. So Paul was born a Roman citizen, which was to be very significant indeed later in his life.

At the same time he was brought up steeped in his Jewish heritage, became a Pharisee and went to train under the Rabbi Gamaliel, a very famous Pharisee, a teacher of the Law. Paul describes himself as very zealous for the Law. So we have somebody of profound intellect, who knows his Jewish Scriptures inside out, who is also a Roman citizen, and who was born and brought up in that cultural melting pot of Asia Minor — Greek-speaking, as well as Hebrew-speaking, and probably also Latin-speaking. He tells us that he was studying in Jerusalem, that he was outraged by what the early Christians were saying about Jesus and that he was one of their opponents — a persecutor of the Church.

Paul tells us that he was actually involved with arresting and persecuting Christian leaders when he had some experience of Christ during the mid-thirties on the road to Damascus. We will look at this event a little later.

There then follows a period of about ten years when we don't know exactly what he was doing, but he was obviously growing in his understanding and his faith, and towards the end of the forties he starts

---

Facts about Paul from the Bible Accounts

Acts 21.39 — 'I am a Jew, from Tarsus in Cilicia.'

Acts 22.27 — The tribune said, 'Are you a Roman citizen?' Paul answered, 'Yes.'

Acts 22.3 — Paul spoke to them in Hebrew: 'I was brought up in this city at the feet of Gamaliel.'

Acts 23.6 — Paul cried out in the council, 'Brethren, I am a Pharisee, a son of Pharisees.'

1 Corinthians 15.9 — 'I am the least of the apostles, unfit to be called an apostle, because I persecuted the Church of God.'

---

writing letters to some of the churches which he has founded. So we assume that in the previous decade he was involved in missionary work, founding churches. In particular, he was working out there in the area he knew, in Asia Minor, in Greek-speaking Asian cities, founding churches of Jews and Gentiles who believed in Jesus.

Gentile: anyone who is not a Jew. There was a great deal of debate in the very early Church about whether Jesus, a Jew, came for the Gentiles as well, and whether a Gentile believer should become a Jew to be a true Christian. Paul believed the gospel was for all people (Rom. 3.29, 30). In the book of Acts, Peter needs a vision from God to persuade him to go to preach to a Gentile centurion, Cornelius (Acts 10).

We don't know exactly when or how Paul died: the letters just stop. Early Christian tradition says that like many of the second generation of Christian leaders he died in Rome, quite possibly during Nero's persecutions in the sixties.

Paul's Writings

Paul's importance is as the author of a large number of letters, placed in the New Testament after the Gospels, written by him to various churches, some of which he founded in Corinth, in Galatia, in Philippi — and in other key Greek and Roman cities like Rome.

Thirteen letters are ascribed to Paul in the New Testament. Of these, scholars today usually accept seven letters as genuinely his — Romans, 1 and 2 Corinthians, Galatians, Philippians, 1 Thessalonians and Philemon — while three are often seen as belonging to later Pauline tradition (1 and 2 Timothy, and Titus). There is continuing debate about the remaining three epistles (Ephesians, Colossians and 2 Thessalonians) which may be from Paul himself, or one of his followers or assistants, writing in his name.

The problem with reading Paul's letters is that it is like one half of a telephone conversation. We have all been annoyed by people who disturb us when we are working, or on the train, by chatting away on their mobile phones. Your attention is caught, but you can only hear one half of the conversation, and you have to work out, 'If that was the answer, what was the question?' Reading Paul's letters is like that. Nowhere in these letters does he set out to write a systematic theology, a summary of the whole of Christian belief. He writes letters in response to letters that the leaders of these churches have written to him, to ask him 'What shall we do about this, or that?' He writes back and tells them how much he cares for them, and assures them of his prayers, and then delves into explanations of whatever they have written to him about. So you always have to ask yourself, 'If this was the answer, what was the question?'

In the letter to the Galatians, which is one of the earliest letters of Paul, he begins 'Paul, an apostle sent, not by human commission or by human authorities, but through Jesus Christ and God the Father who raised him from the dead, to all the churches in Galatia' (Gal. 1.1-2).

Apostle: someone who is sent to represent somebody else: emissary is another translation, or agent, ambassador, representative.

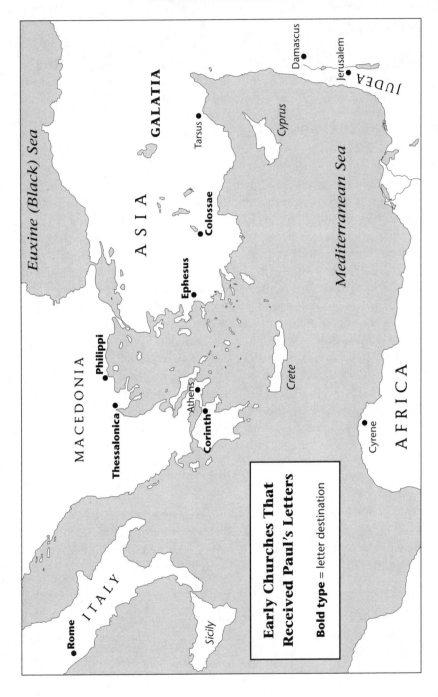

Early Churches That Received Paul's Letters

Bold type = letter destination

Paul is very clear that he was an apostle sent directly by God. He goes on to say that he is astonished that the churches are deserting the gospel of Christ and going into what he describes as a perversion of it. As you read through the letter, you begin to see that Paul is arguing that to be a Christian it is not necessary to be circumcised — to become Jewish, to keep the Law of Moses. So if that is the answer, the question must have been about a debate going on in Galatia between Jewish Christians and Gentile Christians. The Jewish Christians were saying to the non-Jewish Christians that they had to be circumcised, and they had to keep the dietary laws: in fact, they had to become Jewish if they wanted to be Christian. Paul is answering that and saying, in effect, that you don't.

Paul's Experience of Jesus

In this context, Paul explains how he has experienced his Jewishness and its relationship with Christianity. 'You will have heard about my earlier life in Judaism. I was violently persecuting the church of God and trying to destroy it. I advanced in Judaism beyond many people of my own age: I was far more zealous for the traditions of my ancestors. But when God called me through his grace, he revealed his Son to me, that I might proclaim him among the Gentiles [. . .] I didn't go to the human authorities, I didn't go up to the other apostles in Jerusalem' (Gal. 1.13-17). Then he moves forward fourteen years to an argument he had with Peter about whether Gentiles should be circumcised.

This passage in Galatians is the nearest we get to Paul describing his so-called 'conversion experience'. That, however, is a very unhelpful term because Paul wasn't converted: he was already a believer in God, having been brought up Jewish as we have seen. His experience is better described as a revelation, or Paul's revelatory experience. That is how he sees it. The same God and Father that he had worshipped all his life revealed to Paul that he was present in the person of Jesus.

In the book of Acts of the Apostles we find a fuller version of this event. The book of Acts is an account written probably by Luke, the author of the third Gospel, of the events of the first three decades of the Christian Church, particularly those concerning Paul. In Acts chapter 9, (and re-told in chapters 22 and 26), we read about Paul travelling to Damascus in order to oppose, with his keen intellect, the teaching of the

81

Christians who were saying that the Messiah had come. His goal was to arrest them and bring them back to Jerusalem to appear before the priests. Along the way he saw a very bright light, fell off his horse, and heard a voice asking him, 'Saul' (his Hebrew name was Saul), 'Saul, why do you persecute me?' He says, 'Who are you Lord?' and the reply is 'I am Jesus who you are persecuting.' This is a well-known story, and has passed into the language as 'a Damascus Road experience' (Acts 9.1-9).

The other passage in which Paul refers to himself is the list of resurrection appearances in 1 Corinthians 15.3, where he is talking about the importance of the resurrection. It is a very early passage, with the technical term I referred to before — 'I handed on to you as of first importance what I in turn had received': in other words he is saying this is a piece of very early tradition, which was already in coded form to be learned off by heart, and he is passing it on. 'Christ died for our sins, he was buried, he was raised according to the scriptures, he appeared to Peter, to the twelve, to five hundred, to James, to all the apostles, and last of all he appeared also to me. I am the least of the apostles, unfit to be called an apostle, because I persecuted the church of God. But by the grace of God I am what I am.'

So Paul sees the appearance of Jesus to him on the Damascus Road as a kind of post-resurrection experience.

Paul, Judaism and the Jewish Law

It has become common, in the last century or two, to interpret Paul in terms of what is now called the Lutheran experience. Martin Luther, who became a key person in the Reformation, was a Roman Catholic monk who was oppressed by a sense of his own sin and guilt, despite the fact that he was a monk and obeyed all the rules. He was working on a commentary on Paul's letter to the Romans, in which Paul explains how God, in Jesus, has set us free from sin and guilt. Suddenly, although he had been a Christian all his life, Luther appreciated this truth for the first time in a way which applied to himself, and that experience was very influential in the thinking of the Reformation.

Because Luther's interpretation of Paul has been absolutely crucial, particularly within Protestant reformed interpretation of Paul over the last few centuries, the idea that developed was almost that Luther

---

The Reformation

Through the sixteenth century, various movements arose in Europe seeking 'reform' within the Roman Catholic Church, wanting less control from Rome or the Pope and focusing more on the Bible. Eventually various 'protesting' groups separated from the church and, under leaders like Luther in Germany and Calvin in Switzerland, began what came to be called the 'Protestant' churches. Unfortunately, this period was also marked by religious bloodshed and warfare. The Reformation had an enormous impact, for good and ill, on the development of Europe.

---

was repeating Paul's experience. Very often you will read that Paul was brought up a strict Jew, had a desire to serve God but was consumed by sin and by guilt, realized that the Law was not going to satisfy him, and then had this 'conversion'.

The problem is that nowhere in Paul's letters does he actually say that he found the Judaism of his day, and of his own previous life, unsatisfactory, or that it hadn't helped him. Quite the reverse. He says, in the passage I just quoted, 'I advanced beyond everybody of my own day' (Gal. 1.14). E. P. Sanders, the author of a number of huge books on Palestinian Judaism, points out that we must be very careful not to read Palestinian Judaism of the first century through the eyes of post-Reformation theology. He warns against the way in which post-Reformation Christians will often see keeping the Law as a bad thing, from which Christians are set free. Sanders reminds us how for Jews then, as now, the keeping of the Law is a joyous and good thing. It is the gift of God, not an evil thing from which to be set free.

Again, we could look at Philippians 3.4-17, where Paul is describing the argument with Jewish Christians with whom he is in debate:

Beware of these people. They claim that they are good Jews telling you to be circumcised. If anyone has any reason to be confident in human reasons, I have more. I was circumcised on the eighth day,

I'm a member of the people of Israel, I'm of the tribe of Benjamin, I'm a Hebrew born of Hebrews — as to the law, a Pharisee, as to zeal, a persecutor of the church, as to righteousness under the law, blameless.

In other words, 'I kept the law: it was working.' He doesn't say, 'I couldn't keep the law'; instead he says 'I was blameless.' 'But all of that,' he continues, 'I have come to regard as loss because of Christ. I regard everything as rubbish' (or even, in Greek, 'dung'), 'because of the surpassing value of knowing Christ Jesus my Lord, that I might gain Christ, and be found in him, not having a righteousness of my own that comes through the law, but one which comes through faith in Christ. I want to know Christ and the power of his resurrection.'

In other words, Paul is not apologizing in any shape or form for his Jewishness, his upbringing or his learning. He is saying that what he found in Christ was not a replacement, but the culmination of that upbringing. Now, even though he has all those qualifications, they are nothing in his eyes, because of the surpassing worth of what he discovered in Christ. So it is important that we do not project modern Christian experience onto Paul. We need to perceive of him as a very zealous Pharisee who yet finds that same God speaking to him in Jesus.

Paul's Christology

The Impact of Paul's Doctrinal Understanding

How can we best appreciate Paul's doctrinal understanding of the significance of Jesus' life, death and resurrection, what we might call 'the whole Christ event'? He says remarkably little about Jesus' actual human life. He doesn't spend very much time quoting the words or teachings of Jesus — and in fact once or twice when he does, they are teachings that we don't have anywhere in the Gospels, which is probably interesting. We think that little books about Jesus' teaching were circulating around the first-century Mediterranean, and that most Christians would have access to them. Paul is actually not very interested in quoting what Jesus taught, or seeing him as a great moral teacher, or healer. Paul takes all that for granted. He may well, in his teaching, of course, have covered all of that, but in his letters he is really focusing all the time on the 'life, death and resurrection Christ event', as though it is all one thing. For Paul it is the key pivot of the ages.

In the Hebrew Scriptures, you read about the original creation when all was well, and the story of Adam and Eve. Adam means 'ground' or 'earth' and Eve means 'life' — the symbolic parents of all. They reject God, and sin against him, and are banished from paradise (Gen. 2–3). Then comes 'this age', an age dominated by sin and death, when all human beings similarly reject God. But throughout the whole of the Hebrew Scriptures there are these prophecies of another age to come, sometimes referred to as the Kingdom of God, when God will bring the whole universe back to himself. So we have two ages — 'this age' and 'the age to come'.

Christ as the Pivot of the Ages

God put this power to work in Christ when he raised him from the dead and seated him at his right hand in the heavenly places, far above all rule and authority and power and dominion, and above every name that is named, not only in this age but also in the age to come.

(Ephesians 1.20-21)

What Paul finds really significant about Jesus was not anything to do with what he said or did, but that in his life, death and resurrection, the age to come has broken into the present age, and that Jesus is God's agent. Jesus is the means by which all the hopes and anticipations of the Jewish people about the age to come is now being made available through the death and resurrection of Christ. That's his dominant theme.

Centrality of the Resurrection

Therefore the resurrection is central. This is clear from 1 Corinthians 15, a very early passage where Paul is handing on what is known about the appearances of the risen Christ to various people. Having established that list of appearances (vv. 3-11), he then goes on to say in verses 12-19 that the resurrection is the absolutely key issue. To paraphrase him slightly, he says: 'If there is no resurrection, we are most of all to be pitied. Our preaching is in vain, your faith is in vain, and we will even be found to be misrepresenting God if we say God raised Christ from the dead, and he didn't. If Christ is not raised, your faith is futile, and you are still in your sins and in death. But in fact, because Christ has been raised from the dead, everything else follows from this.'

He draws a parallel between Adam as the first man, and Christ as the last man, the *eschatos* man, the man to do with the end. As Adam disobeyed God, so Christ obeyed God. Through Adam came death, through Christ came life. Through Adam there was sin, through Christ comes forgiveness. He builds up this parallel all the way through his theology, that eventually all things will be subjected to Christ, who will then bring them all to God (1 Cor. 15.20-57; Rom. 5.12-21). That is the key issue for him.

So what Paul is interested in is what God has *done* in Jesus more than in who Jesus *is*. He has a very high understanding of who Jesus is, not so much because of what Jesus did, but because of what God did in him, in his death and his resurrection.

Key Structures of Paul's Theology

After Christology, there are three further themes that run through Paul's theology. Theology is about your understanding of God. Paul doesn't set out to write a guide to his theology in three easy steps. He's writing letters to people, and we have to deduce his theology from it.

The Eschatological Dimension

The first is what we call eschatology, the end. For him, Christ is the *eschatos* Adam, the last Adam (Greek *eschatos* means last or final). There is this eschatological dimension to his theology, that God has inaugurated the age to come in his saving work in Christ, but it is not yet complete. In most of the eschatological material in the Hebrew Scriptures, the idea is that God will bring to an end *(eschaton)* this current age with a cosmic cataclysm, the day of the Lord, which brings judgement. 'The end of the world is at hand', these writings insist: it will be destroyed and replaced with a new world and a new universe. What Paul is talking about is an overlapping of the age to come with the age now. Actually, God doesn't want to destroy his creation, his handiwork. So this age will come to an end, but the age beyond the end has broken into the age now, and we live in between the times. We exist in an overlap between this present age, which is passing, and the future age which is coming. So there is this tension always in Paul's thoughts between the 'now' and the 'not yet'. In the here and now we are already experiencing all the benefits of the end times, but the end is not yet fully realized. So we are living between the times, in balance.

The Effect of the Future upon This Present Age

Let us take just one example of this, in his letter to the Romans, chapter 13, where Paul begins with very basic ethical instructions about the state. This is remarkable considering he was writing to the Roman Christians during the reign of Nero — a little before the widespread persecutions, but Nero was never a particularly pleasant emperor to live under. Paul explains that everybody should be subject to the governing authorities. There is a whole section about obeying the state in verses 1-7.

This is a passage which Christians living under Hitler had to grapple with, and equally Christians resisting apartheid: the former Archbishop of Cape Town in the apartheid era, Desmond Tutu, talks of doing Bible studies with President De Klerk who said, 'Look, it says here in Romans 13 that you have to obey me: why don't you?' Tutu's answer was that God instituted human authorities for 'good conduct' (13.3) — not for terror like apartheid.

Then in verses 8-10, Paul gives other ethical instructions about owing no one anything except loving one another because the one who loves has fulfilled the Law. Then he quotes a number of the Ten Commandments: You shall not commit adultery, you shall not steal, you shall not covet — they are all summed up, he says, in the command 'Love your neighbour as yourself'. Love, he says, is the fulfilling of the Law.

Then suddenly he moves from basic instruction to say 'Now is the moment to wake up. Salvation is nearer than when we first believed. The night is far gone, the day is breaking, lay aside the works of darkness, put on the armour of light' (Rom. 13.11-14). In other words, even those basic and contemporary ethical instructions he was giving about obeying the state, and paying taxes, are motivated because we are living between the times. It's not just about being a good moral teacher for the now. Even that basic moral teaching is driven by Paul's belief that the End of all things is upon us, is happening, and is breaking in now. And that is why you should do everything from basics such as paying your taxes and keeping the laws, through to loving one another — because the End is breaking in.

Three Tenses of Salvation

We can talk about the three tenses of Paul's idea of salvation — past, present and future. From Paul's point of view you can say 'I have been saved because Christ died on the cross; I am being saved, I am in the process of being brought into the Kingdom of God; and I will be saved at the end of all things when the Kingdom is finally completed in Christ.' Again we see this overlapping eschatology. For Paul, what allows the Age to come to burst into the present is the life, death and resurrection of Jesus.

Participation in Christ through His Death

Paul is clear about Christ's sacrificial death. In 1 Corinthians 15, again, the passage about the resurrection we looked at earlier, he says, 'Christ died for our sins.' At the heart of Jewish belief was this idea of sacrifice, that you could take a pure animal, you could sacrifice it, or give it to the priests in the temple to sacrifice it on your behalf, and that, as it were, the animal pays the price for your sins. You may have broken the Law, your blood deserves to be shed, but God provides for you a way out. God provides a sacrifice and accepts the blood of the animal, so you get the innocence of the animal given to you. A lamb was a particularly important animal in this regard, and regularly we come across the idea of Jesus as the Lamb of God in the New Testament.

Sacrifice in the Old Testament and the New Testament

The Passover sacrifice: Exodus 12.23-27; Mark 14.12

Other sacrifices: Leviticus 3.1-11; Numbers 7.17; 1 Kings 8.5, 62-64

Jesus as sacrifice: Romans 3.25; Hebrews 10.11-12; 1 John 2.2

Jesus as the sacrificed Lamb: Revelation 5.6-10

In Paul's thought, as he sees the whole of the Law summed up in the life of Christ, he also sees the whole of the temple, cult, sacrificial system as summed up in the death of Christ on the cross. In the crucifixion, it was like the Lamb of God being slaughtered. It is seen as an exchange: he takes our sin, he gives us his life.

Ransomed from Slavery

Do you not know that if you yield yourselves to anyone as obedient slaves, you are slaves of the one you obey, either of sin, which leads to death, or of obedience, which leads to righteousness? [. . .]

But now that you have been set free from sin and have become slaves of God, the return you get is sanctification, and its end, eternal life.

(Romans 6.16, 22)

Running through this we also find the picture of Christ having ransomed us. Paul uses the picture of a slave who belongs to a master and someone comes along to buy the slave and set the slave free. This is what Christ has done: he comes to us while we are enslaved to sin; he pays the price we cannot pay and sets us free. That's also a very important way of understanding Christ in Paul's thought. But it is important to remember that these are only pictures or metaphors — sacrifice and ransom — for the reality Christ has gained for us by his death.

The Christian Community as the Body of Christ

For Paul, the really key idea is what happens next, which is the new life in Christ. It is because of his sacrifice we can have a share, not just in his death, but also in his new life. There is what we might call a shift of allegiance and status. In the middle of the letter to the Romans, in chapters 5–8, we read a clear statement of Paul's theology of this participation and solidarity. The Jewish scriptures have the idea of being 'in Abraham', or 'in Israel', where Israel is a person but is also a people. Paul calls upon this idea and says there are two kinds of humanity: those who are 'in Adam', and those who are 'in Christ'. Through Adam and Eve there is the old humanity, and in Christ there is the new humanity. He is saying that all human beings participate in Adam, all human beings share in Adam's sin. All human beings have rejected God the way Adam did. All human beings will die as Adam did.

But there is a new humanity being created by God in Christ. Christ did not sin, Christ was obedient. As Christ died, so we have all died with him, and as Christ is in the resurrection life, so we live the resurrection life in him. Therefore we should be starting to live in the here and now as though we were already in the age to come. We have died to sin, and we cannot therefore live in it. So he says in 2 Corinthians 5.17, 'If anyone is in Christ they are a new creation.' The whole of creation is already being renewed by the life, death and resurrection of Christ, and people have the option to transfer out from being in the old humanity in Adam, and transfer into the new humanity in Christ.

We can see here the overlapping of the ages. At one moment Paul is saying, 'There is no condemnation for those who are in Christ Jesus: you are now free' (Rom. 8.1-2), and then he says, 'Live as though that were true, live that out. Let not sin reign in your life' (Rom. 6.2, 12). In other words he is saying that ontologically, theologically, eschatologically, you are already reigning with God in the highest heavens. Practically, you are still in the world, in the flesh and you still make mistakes, and you still sin, but you should start to live as though the theological reality were the present reality. If you have died to sin in Christ, you must live out that new life now.

Paul sees that when people are baptized, they are drowned, they die, and they share in the death of Christ upon the cross (Rom. 6.1-11). When they come out of the waters of baptism, then they share the new life of the resurrection. This is why he can come up with the incredible idea that there is a new creation in Christ. In 2 Corinthians 5.17-19 he says, 'If anyone is in Christ there is a new creation. Everything old has passed away, everything has become new. All this has come from God, who has reconciled us to himself through Christ, that is, in Christ God was reconciling the world to himself.' So there is a completely new era.

The Christian community is therefore a corporate group, a body. He uses this image, 'the body of Christ', and says that all the individual Christians together make up Christ's body, and Christ is the head. Therefore to be baptized into Christ is to become part of his body here on earth, and that body takes priority over all human relationships, allegiances and so on (1 Cor. 12.12-13).

Breaking Down the Barriers

All One in Christ Jesus

As many of you as were baptized into Christ have clothed yourselves in Christ. In Christ Jesus you are all children of God. There is no longer Jew or Greek, there is no longer slave or free: there is no longer male or female: you are all one in Christ Jesus.

(Galatians 3.26-28)

In this extraordinary piece, in a very early stage of Paul's theology, that single sentence from Galatians 3.26-28 cuts right through the social divisions of the first century. Obviously, there was the hugely important division between male and female: only men could be Roman citizens, only men could be Greek citizens, and a Jewish prayer ran 'Blessed are you, Lord God of the Universe, that you have not made me a woman.' Now Paul says, 'In Christ there is neither male nor female'. Equally, hugely central to any sociological understanding of the ancient world is the difference between slaves and free. Slaves could be bought and sold, only free men could be citizens. Now Paul says, 'no longer slave or free'. Then of course, the division that he has been grappling with, Paul himself being Jewish, Jesus being Jewish and all the early

Christian believers being Jewish, is whether believers who came from outside the community had to be circumcised and keep the Jewish Law to become Christian. He says, 'You are neither Jew nor Greek, you are all one in Christ.'

It has to be admitted that the Christian Church has played its part in the oppression of slaves, of women, and of the Jewish people over the last two thousand years and has not always worked out that insight. But what Paul is saying in his theology is that there is this new humanity which Christ has brought in which transcends all divisions. It's true at one level, theologically, but it has to be put into practice, and it has taken us a long time to work it out.

Throughout his letters, Paul has this overriding concern for unity in Christ. He writes to the Corinthians that he has heard that there are lots of groups of them arguing with one another, and some are saying, 'I belong to Paul', 'I belong to the Peter group', and others are saying 'I belong to Apollos', and he says, 'No, you are all one in Christ' (1 Cor. 1.10-31). Later on, in 1 Corinthians 12, he again uses this image of a body, and he talks about legs and eyes and arms and ears, and says if you were all legs, where would the hearing be? You are all individually members of Christ, the body, with many different gifts and many different ways of being, but you all share growing up into Christ, the head of the body (1 Corinthians 12.12-27).

The Cosmic Christ

Paul's understanding of Jesus is cosmic in the proper sense of the word. In this historical person who was only a few years older than Paul, who lived and died not far away, whom Paul had been persecuting, Paul came to see summed up all the hopes of Israel. More than that, he says that the human Jesus was actually also the Christ of God, who existed before time. He came from God in the same sense as the Jewish ideas about Wisdom, he lived and died a human life and a human death and was raised to new life. In those very human events, God has brought about a transformation which reverberates through the cosmos.

New Testament Views of Jesus

So far we have seen that the life and death of Jesus, and whatever happened afterwards, were the crucial catalyst for the production of the books of the New Testament by his early followers. In their different ways, both the four Gospels and the letters of Paul (who wrote a large part of the rest of the New Testament) put Jesus at their centre. Looking at them together, we are shown complementary insights into Jesus himself and the impact of his life.

In this final chapter on the New Testament views of Jesus, we need to look at whether Paul thought Jesus was God, and at some other views in the rest of the New Testament. It will also be instructive to ask the questions, 'What can we know about Jesus' own self-understanding? Did Jesus think of himself as God?'

Does Paul Think of Jesus as God?

At no point does Paul stop being Jewish, and at no point does he stop being monotheist. As we saw in the first chapter, this of course is the major debate between Christians and the other monotheistic religions such as Islam and Judaism. Within a monotheistic framework, where there is only one God and God alone, the Christian concept of the Trinity is seen as either nonsensical or blasphemous.

Given this, it is amazing how enormous Paul's understanding of Jesus is: he asserts that all the promises of God are fulfilled in Jesus, that he has come from God, that he has gone back to God, and that everything will be subjected to him. In Jesus, God has fulfilled his promises to Israel and inaugurated the new age to come.

And yet, it is interesting that Paul is reticent to use the 'God' word to describe Jesus. He uses the word 'Lord' all the way through, and he takes Old Testament passages where God is described as Lord, and applies them quite happily to Jesus. For example, in Philippians 2.11 he says 'every tongue shall confess him as Lord', applying to Jesus what Isaiah 45.23 says about God. So to all intents and purposes he puts Jesus on a level footing with God, and yet there are only two or three verses where he actually calls Jesus 'God'.

One of these is Romans 9.5, and even here the punctuation makes the true meaning of the verse problematic. Paul is talking about his pain and anguish over his Jewish brothers and sisters who do not believe in Jesus. He says, 'I wish I were cursed — I am prepared to be cut off from Christ — for the sake of my own people', if only they would come to Christ. He continues, 'They are Israelites: to them belongs the adoption, the Law, the worship, the glory' and so on, 'and from them according to the flesh comes the Christ who is over all, God blessed for ever'. The debate about how you punctuate that sentence focuses on whether Paul describes Christ as 'God to be blessed for ever', or whether the sentence about the inheritance of Israel stops at Christ and concludes with a paean of praise to God. Scholars love this kind of debate, given that there is no punctuation in the manuscripts! Paul possibly does call Jesus 'God' here — but in the context of an outpouring of praise.

There are two other passages, 2 Thessalonians 1.12 and Colossians 2.2, where he describes Christ as God. But generally, he seems to talk about God as Father of our Lord Jesus Christ and Jesus Christ as Lord: he clearly exalts Jesus to the status of God, but somehow still seems to distinguish God the Father as being separate from Jesus.

One of his favourite descriptions of the relationship is the idea of God sending his Son. This is specifically spelled out in Galatians 4.4-6, Romans 8.3, and Philippians 2.5-11, but it really runs as a thread all the way through Paul's thought. In the last chapter we looked at the little hymn in Philippians 2 where it talks about Jesus who, though he was equal with God, did not count equality with God as something to be grasped at, but humbled himself, took human form and died a human death. So Paul sees Jesus as the Son of God, whom God sends, as all the prophecies foretold in Hebrew Scriptures about God sending Wisdom.

His favourite word in relation to Jesus is 'Lord': he uses it some 250 times in his letters. Of course, normally Jewish readers of the Scriptures would only use the word 'Lord' to refer to God. Yet Paul is quite happy to use the word 'Lord' of Jesus, and he also uses the phrase 'the Son of God' about seventeen times.

Children of God

All who are led by the Spirit of God are children of God. You did not receive a spirit of slavery, to fall back into fear, but a spirit of adoption. When we cry Abba, Father, it is the Spirit bearing witness with our spirit that we are children of God, and if children, then heirs with God and joint-heirs with Christ.

(Romans 8.14-17)

Furthermore, he describes the way in which Jesus, as the Son of God, brings human beings into the relationship of being 'the children of God' (Rom. 8.14-17). He is using the idea that human beings are not able to live up to their destiny of being the children of God and have said 'No' to God all the way down through history. But Christ is the perfect Son of God who then brings all other human beings into that participation of being the children of God. He also uses other great images from Hebrew Scriptures, of Jesus as the Last Adam (contrasting with the first Adam), of Jesus being the Wisdom of God, as we have already seen, or Jesus being the Saviour.

So even if Paul is reticent about using the word 'God' to describe Jesus, what is clear in his thinking all the way through is that Jesus functions like God. Jesus does all the things that God does. Jesus is involved in the creation in the first place, Jesus is involved in salvation, and he is involved at the end of all things.

In the next few chapters we shall see how the difference between 'function' and 'being' are worked out in the world of Greek philosophy — what Jesus does and who Jesus is. Hebrew thought is very functional, has a lot to do with verbs and actions, and wants to know what something *does:* the Greeks are very ontological, very interested in being, and want to know what something *is.* Once you read the New Testament taking into account its Greek environment, you get fairly quickly into the debate of the second, third and fourth centuries, into the Greek philosophy about being, and that leads to all the debates which give us the classical doctrines of the Trinity and the incarnation.

But Paul is thinking in a much more functional way, and hasn't yet had to address the question of 'Who exactly do you think Jesus is, and what is his relationship with God?' All Paul says is that Jesus functions like God. Paul's Christology is probably best summed up in the phrase 'God was in Christ, reconciling the world to himself' (2 Cor. 5.19). In Christ, God is active, and in the person of Jesus, God was acting here among us to bring us to himself.

The Later Pauline Letters: The Pastoral Letters

These letters, two of which were written to someone called Timothy, and one written to somebody called Titus, may have been written by Paul in his latter years, or may have been written by one of his secretaries or associates. They seem to presume a situation a bit later than the letters written in Paul's missionary period: now the Church seems to have settled down more and the so-called 'pastoral' letters are concerned with how to be a minister and care for the church of God.

1 and 2 Timothy

Background to Timothy

Timothy came from Lystra in Asia Minor and became a companion of Paul on his missionary journeys (see Acts 16.1-3, 17.14, 18.5, 20.4). He is often linked with Paul in the opening greetings of letters (2 Cor. 1.1; Phil. 1.1) or in the final greetings (Rom. 16.21). He was also used by Paul as his envoy (1 Cor. 4.17).

Here, too, it is clear that 'Christ Jesus came into the world to save sinners' (1 Tim. 1.15). Again in 1 Timothy 2.5-6, we read the same idea: 'there is one God and one Mediator between God and humankind, Christ himself, being human, who gave himself as a ransom for all'. At the end of the next passage, there comes another of these bits of primitive poetry which we saw in our last chapter, which could be an early hymn or part of a creed:

> He was revealed in flesh, vindicated in Spirit,
> seen by angels, proclaimed among Gentiles,
> believed in throughout the world
> and taken up in glory.
>
> (1 Timothy 3.16)

Again, we see the 'descending/ascending' motif — that Jesus comes from God, takes human form, lives among us and then returns to God.

Titus

This letter is a pastoral letter for the care of the churches in Crete, and contains teaching on the qualities needed for church leaders and bishops (chapter 1), the behaviour of various groups in church (chapter 2) and the right way to behave in this world (chapter 3).

Titus

Titus is another companion of Paul on some of his journeys (see Gal. 2.1-3), also used as an envoy (2 Cor. 7.6-14; 8.6-17) and described as a 'partner and co-worker' (2 Cor. 8.23).

In this letter to Titus, Jesus is actually described in terms of being God and Saviour, 'the glory of our great God and Saviour, Jesus Christ' (Titus 2.13). So these later letters pick up and continue that same Pauline idea of God in Christ, Christ coming into the world to save sinners.

The Rest of the New Testament

The Letter to the Hebrews

We don't know who wrote this long letter, which is more like a sermon or treatise, but it is clearly written to Hebrew Christians, Jews who believed that Christ was the Messiah. It is full of prophecies from the Hebrew Scriptures all the way through, to show the way in which Jesus is the fulfilment of the Hebrew thoughts and hopes.

Hebrews

Although some early Church fathers thought this may have been written by Paul, the style is very different and the author is not named. It describes much of the cult activity in the temple, which was destroyed in 70 CE, and relates how Jesus is superior to all of that.

The central idea is that of the 'heavenly High Priest', and it draws on the imagery of the High Priest and the sacrifices in the temple, to say that all these Old Testament pictures are fulfilled in Jesus too. It begins with its central Christological point, which is that Jesus is the Son through whom everything was created. 'Long ago, God spoke to our ancestors in many and different ways by the prophets. In these last days he has spoken to us by a Son, whom he appointed heir of all things and through whom he created the world. He is the reflection of God's glory, the exact imprint of God's very being, and he sustains all things by his powerful word' (Heb. 1.1-3). That is to say, the same God who has spoken down through the prophets has now revealed himself supremely in Jesus. What God is, Jesus is.

At the same time the writer continues to distinguish between Jesus and God. Jesus is above all the angels. Sometimes the writer prefers to use the words 'apostle' and 'High Priest' to describe Jesus. 'Look at Jesus, the apostle and High Priest of our confession. He was faithful as Moses was faithful' (Heb. 3.1). Right the way through chapters 4 to 10 he works out this idea that Jesus is the High Priest for ever. Here he calls on the priestly imagery in all the books of Moses which talk about the High Priest, and he says that all that the High Priest was, Jesus now is. Jesus has gone into the heavenly Temple to offer the ultimate sacrifice (Heb. 8–10).

At the same time, he also argues that Jesus is the victim, the sacrifice. Whereas the High Priest went into the Holy of Holies and took the blood of the sacrificial animal, what Jesus has done is to enter into the presence of God with his own blood (Heb. 9.11–10.25). Here we have in Jesus the extraordinary combination of both priest and victim — the High Priest who makes the sacrifice, and yet also the animal which is killed.

Alongside that very 'high' view of Jesus, there is the idea that he entered into our world to experience the 'low' side: sharing our humanity, temptation ('tempted as we are', Heb. 2.14-18; 4.14-16) and weakness (Heb. 2). Jesus is therefore both the Author of salvation and the example to follow (2.10; 5.7-9). The letter ends with the statement, 'Jesus Christ is the same, yesterday, today and for ever' (Heb. 13.8).

In many ways, what the writer of the letter to Hebrews was doing is nothing different from what Paul was doing, which is to say that all that God has done in the past for the Jewish people has now come true in Jesus. Yet at the same time what he says is quite different, because he is writing for a different group. Paul was writing to his early converts, a mixture of Jews and Greeks, and he uses a set of arguments that this group will understand. The writer of the epistle to the Hebrews uses all the concepts which *Jewish* Christian believers will understand: he claims that everything they have known since childhood about sacrifice and priesthood is also summarized in Christ. This idea is not systematically worked out at this stage: that happens in the centuries afterwards, which we will look at in the next few chapters. But each writer has the idea that Jesus is at the centre, and has to apply it in different ways for the different audiences.

The Letter of James

This is a very brief letter with a lot of practical instructions about ethics and the way people should be living. It has practically no doctrinal theology in it at all. Instead James gives instructions about not just believing things, but actually living out faith in practice: going to visit widows and orphans, caring for the poor, not showing favouritism to the rich and those sorts of things. He echoes traditional Jewish teaching about ethics and living faith out in practical ways.

James

Perhaps a brother of Jesus (Mark 6.3), a leader of the church in Jerusalem (Acts 15.13; Gal. 1.19, 2.9).

This letter doesn't have a very explicit theology of Christ, because it doesn't set out to do that. The Christology here is implied: the ethical instructions are based on the understanding that Jesus is a teacher, and he is described in 1.1 and 2.1 as 'the Lord Jesus Christ'. 'When you show favouritism', he says about people who take the rich to places of honour in the assembly, 'do you really think this is the work of someone who believes in the glorious Lord Jesus Christ?' He places Jesus as Lord with God in 'bless the Lord and Father' in 3.9. Although he doesn't have a worked-out Christology on the page, James keeps calling Jesus Lord and so shares the same ideas which we saw in Paul and in Hebrews.

The Letter of Jude

Jude

A 'brother of James' (1.1), traditionally identified as another brother of Jesus (see Mark 6.3).

The other letters in the New Testament canon are all quite brief. One of the shortest, Jude, is full of Jewish ideas, and yet, like Paul, the writer doesn't hesitate to call Jesus 'Lord'. In verse 1 he says he is writing to 'those who are called, beloved in God the Father and kept for Jesus Christ'. He talks of 'our only Master and Lord, Jesus Christ' in verse 4. Then there's a lot of material about false angels and false teachers, and about what will happen on the day of judgement, and here we find the idea that all he says about the archangel Michael is summed up in Jesus. There is also an early idea of the Trinity in verses 20-21, where he exhorts his readers: 'Pray in the Holy Spirit, keep yourselves in the love of God, wait for the mercy of our Lord Jesus Christ unto eternal life.' When he ends the letter he does it with an ascription of praise, 'to the only God our Saviour through Jesus Christ our Lord be glory, majesty, dominion and authority, before all time and now and for ever' (v. 25). So here again we have a balance between an indication of a difference between God and Jesus, and the fact that everything we know about God is coming in and through Jesus.

The Letters of Peter

Peter

The author is called 'Peter, an apostle of Jesus Christ' in 1 Peter 1.1. This letter was written either by the apostle Peter himself in the 60s or by a colleague later; his concern for church leaders (5.1) fits in with the apostle's ministry.

Peter writes to a group of Christians who are being persecuted, and talks to them about church organization in that context, and how they can cope with suffering and pain. Again, when he talks about Jesus, he is clearly describing Jesus as Christ and Lord, but he wants to make Jesus relevant to their situation too. So in 1 Peter 2.21-25 he talks about Jesus as a suffering servant. Paul has said that in Christ there is neither slave nor free, as we saw in the last chapter, but many of the early Christians were slaves and were being abused horribly by their pagan masters. So Peter says in 1 Peter 2.18, 'Slaves, you must accept the authority of your human masters,' and his reasoning comes in verses 21-25: 'To this you have been called because Christ also suffered for you. Jesus committed no sin: when he was abused, he did not return abuse, when he suffered, he did not threaten. He bore our sins in his body on the cross, so that free from sin we might live to righteousness. By his wounds we are healed. You were going astray like sheep, but now you have returned to the Shepherd and Guardian of your souls.' A new idea is developed when Jesus is described in 2.4-6 as being the cornerstone of a new Temple. Peter calls him Lord at 3.15 ('sanctify Christ as Lord'), and in chapter 4 talks about how he suffered in the flesh (4.1), and finally defines him as the 'Chief Shepherd' at the end of the letter (5.4). The second letter of Peter begins with 'To those who received the faith through the righteousness of our God and Saviour Jesus Christ', and Jesus is described regularly throughout this letter as 'the Lord', as in 'Lord and Saviour' (2 Pet. 1.11; 2.20; 3.2).

The Letters of John

John

This John is sometimes identified with the apostle John, writer of the fourth Gospel, since these letters share similar language and vocabulary with that Gospel. However, they arise from a very different situation and were possibly written much later. The author calls himself 'the elder' (2 John 1; 3 John 1) and is thus best seen as a church leader following John's tradition.

These are three very short letters, written in the context of people who are arguing about the significance of Jesus. Clearly the debate here was not about what it means to call Jesus God, or Lord, or Christ, since that is taken for granted (see, for example, 1 John 4.13-15; 2 John 3, 9). Instead in these letters the question was the extent to which Jesus was human. The letters reveal a bitter argument within these churches about which group had the right ideas about Jesus — and which were wrong. John suggests in 1 John 4.2 what the test should be: 'How do we know if somebody is giving a prophecy from God? By this we know the Spirit of God: every spirit which confesses that Jesus Christ has come in the flesh is of God, but every spirit which does not confess Jesus, is not of God.' In other words, it is the recognition that Jesus came 'as a human being among us' which is crucial. Similarly in 2 John 7, 'Many deceivers have gone out who do not confess that Jesus Christ has come in the flesh. Such a person is a deceiver and an antichrist.' He is referring here to a group which became known in the second century as the docetics.

> **Doceticism, docetics**: from the Greek *dokeo* — to seem, or to appear. Docetics believed that the divine Jesus only 'appeared' to be human.

This idea arises from the fact that within Greek thought it was extraordinary to think that God might actually touch physical matter. The idea of God becoming human, from a Greek philosophical point of view, was outrageous. So some people began to argue that Jesus wasn't really human. Jesus was an apparition from God who appeared to be human when he came among us. Equally, they claimed, Jesus didn't die, he just appeared to die. What these letters underline is that it is absolutely crucial that Jesus is human as well as Lord and Christ, and that Christians confess him as having come 'in the flesh'. This was a debate which continued into the second and third centuries as early Christians debated how Jesus could be both God and human. It still has relevance for today, in that some Christians are so keen to stress the divinity of Christ that they never really grapple with his human qualities.

The Revelation to John

> ### Revelation
>
> The author of this book is also called John (1.1, 4, 9; 22.8) with some possible links to the rest of the Johannine tradition. He is often called St John the Divine to distinguish him from the author of the Gospel and of the letters. The book was possibly written in Asia Minor (western Turkey) during the persecutions of the Roman emperor Domitian in the mid 90s.

The book of Revelation, an extraordinary book painted in glorious Technicolor, is an eschatological work — a book about the end times (*eschaton* in Greek). It is also of the type of literature we call 'apocalyptic', where the veil is taken away and the truth is revealed. It is written particularly for people who are suffering for their faith, even to the point of being killed. John encourages them to look up from the earthly dimension, and to see that God is actually still in control. The persecutions they are suffering are what they should expect before the end of all things, when God — and not the Romans or any other brutal state — will triumph. Central to that vision of the end is the glorious Christ.

The book begins with the author having a vision of the Son of Man clothed in a long robe, his hair white as snow, his voice like the rushing of many waters: an extraordinary vision of the resurrected, ascended, glorified Christ (1.12-18). In the course of the book Jesus is described as Christ seven times, regularly as 'Lord' (23 times), and yet the favourite term, used 28 times, is 'the Lamb'. There is a lot of blood flowing in this book, and much of it is the blood of the Lamb who was slain. He is dipped in his own blood at the end (19.13). When the people are suffering and shedding their blood, what they are doing is sharing in the suffering of Christ, who shed his blood for us.

In the same way as we saw that in the letter to the Hebrews, in a Jewish context, Jesus is seen both as High Priest and victim, so here too the writer is a Jewish Christian familiar with the prophetic and apocalyptic tradition. He works out the idea that Jesus is a martyr like many others, the slain one, and yet he is also the Ruler of all. 'The Kingdom of the world is become the Kingdom of our Lord and of his Christ' (11.15). In chapter 19 we read of the final battle between God and evil, where Christ, the Word of God, rides on a white horse. Here you have the words of that great Handel chorus: 'Hallelujah, for the Lord the Almighty reigns, King of Kings, Lord of Lords' — and this is a description of Jesus as King of Kings and Lord of Lords (19.6, 16). He rides out and defeats his enemies as evil is finally destroyed (ch. 20). Then there is a new heaven and a new earth, and the people of God are the Bride of Christ (chs. 21 and 22). At the end John sees a heavenly city, the new Jerusalem. This is an extraordinary vision of the end of all things, and crucial to that vision is the image of Jesus as the one who makes it possible, who conquers through it all, who is the Bridegroom who marries the bride, the people of God (19.9; 21.2, 9). This incredibly rich picture, although in very different language from the rest of the books in the New Testament, is saying again that all our hopes, all our dreams, are made real by God in Christ, changing the world by his death, shedding his blood — and making possible the new age of life with God.

An Overview of the New Testament

So what we have in the New Testament as a whole is a variety of images of Jesus. We have looked at the evidence for the historical Jesus himself — for his life and ministry — and we have seen how the four Gospel pictures of him give us access to four different portraits of the same basic story. Paul takes up the theme, working out in a very rich way what the whole event of Jesus' life, death and resurrection means. After that we have also seen little pen portraits, little cameos in all the other letters in the New Testament, most of which are not specifically about the person of Jesus, but take it for granted that he is Lord, human and divine, Son of God the Father. Ultimately the New Testament culminates in Revelation's amazing cosmic vision.

Jesus' Own Self-Understanding

Lastly, is it possible to learn from the Gospels what Jesus understood to be true about himself? This is, of course, a very complex question. If I ask you, 'What impact has your father had on your life?' you will immediately be aware that some of this impact is conscious and you would talk about it, some you wouldn't mention except to close friends and there is a whole lot more of which you are unaware. Mostly, though, you don't talk about it very much, and acquaintances are often intrigued when they meet your father to see you in a new way, which throws light on some of your characteristics. Our focus when we talk about Jesus' self-understanding is 'Did Jesus think he was God?' Actually, Jesus spoke about his Father and their relationship a great deal. Some of what he says is implied, and we have to read between the lines of the texts to a certain extent, but there are good guidelines there. Also, implicit in Jesus' actions and attitudes we see the characteristics of the Father.

Most scholars' accounts of the historical Jesus note a sense of what I think of as his 'teasing authority'. He frequently uses the oblique phrase 'the Son of Man' to refer to himself, a title which has implications about being the ultimate human being or the representative of the human race. Jesus himself seemed to fight shy of language such as 'Lord', 'Christ', and 'Son of God', perhaps because of the possible military connotations of political leadership, leading troops against the Romans and so on. There is a good example of this kind of evasion where we read of Peter's confession in Mark 8.29. Peter takes the groundbreaking step of identifying Jesus as the Christ, and Jesus' response suggests that Peter has got it right. Yet in the very next verse, he goes back to talking about 'the Son of Man' going up to Jerusalem to suffer and die, and it is very clear that he is still speaking about himself.

It is usually significant when Jesus' original Aramaic language is preserved in the Greek of the New Testament, and there are two places where Aramaic words are very instructive for understanding Jesus' self-awareness. One is the use of the Aramaic phrase 'amen, amen', or 'truly, truly', to introduce his teaching (Matt. 5.18; Mark 3.28; John 3.5). This gives it a new authority, and implies that he was imparting a higher level of teaching. It is not cutting across Moses or the Law, but there is a claim to a new authority. Jesus saw himself as acting on God's behalf, as God's representative, or God's agent in bringing in the Kingdom.

Abba, Father

Jesus said, 'Abba, Father, for you all things are possible; remove this cup from me; yet, not what I want, but what you want.' (Mark 14.36)

'Pray then in this way: "Our Father in heaven, hallowed be your name".' (Matthew 6.9)

The second interesting use is the fact that Jesus referred to God as 'Abba', which was the Aramaic word meaning 'Daddy'. There was something in Jesus' own prayer which struck people very forcibly. He prayed to God with an awareness of a very natural and personal relationship with his Father. Also, in the parables he tells, Jesus puts himself in a different category from other men. For example, in Mark 12.1-12, he tells the story of a vineyard and the tenants who won't give the owner the rent. The owner sends lots of servants who are beaten up by the wicked tenants, and then the owner sends his only son, and the tenants kill him. He's clearly telling the story about his own mission, and it's interesting that he distinguishes himself, 'the beloved Son', from the other prophets.

Jesus also took it upon himself to act in a God-like way. In accepting the poor, the weak, women, Gentiles, lepers and other people considered unimportant by the religious authorities, Jesus was accepting people back into the culture of the people of God without requiring them to go to the temple and make sacrifices. It is very clear that ancient Judaism was a religion of forgiveness, love and grace. Sometimes Christians caricature it as saying 'You have to keep all the law otherwise you are not acceptable', but that is unfair. There is forgiveness, there is redemption — but it is through the system of sacrifice. However, Jesus flings the door wide open, welcoming the wicked into God's Kingdom. He accepts people not because of their sacrifices at the temple, but because of their reaction to him as a person.

These are the sorts of things which indicate Jesus' own particular understanding of what or who he was. At the very least, Jesus had a sense of mission, of being sent from God. He acted like God — giving people life, healing, forgiving sin and accepting outcasts. Yet he also seems to have claimed a special relationship with God. In this he sets the tracks for the New Testament's later reflections on both what he *did* as God's agent and who he *is* in relation to God and to human beings. In this way, both the biblical accounts of Jesus in the New Testament which we have seen in these chapters and the later theological debates which we will cover in Part 2 can be seen as legitimate outworkings of Jesus' own self-consciousness.

The Development of Different Views

It used to be popular, though less so now, to talk about an evolution in our understanding of Jesus from Jewish teacher to Gentile God. Certainly up until the middle of the twentieth century, but occasionally since, some scholars said that Jesus began as a Jewish rabbi, a human teacher of the Law, and gradually as news about him spread out into the Greek world the believers added the idea of the divine man, a saviour figure. In the course of the first century, this thinking runs, Jesus became more and more elevated until eventually he became seen as a Gentile God. This is linked to the idea of later dates for documents with more exalted Christological ideas, like John's Gospel.

'Development is a better analogy than evolution for the genesis of New Testament Christology.'

(C. F. D. Moule, *The Origin of Christology* (Cambridge University Press, 1977), p. 135)

As we have seen, this is an oversimplification which just doesn't work. The roots of the so-called 'high' Christology, seeing Jesus sharing the life of God, are there right at the earliest level within the first communities of Jewish believers, indeed perhaps even in Jesus' own self-understanding. This is not something that gets imported half a century later from a Greek background. It is better, therefore, to talk about the development of Christology, or even of Christologies within the New Testament.

'Perhaps the model of the sun with various beams radiating out from it is more apt than the linear development model.'

(Ben Witherington III, *The Many Faces of the Christ: The Christologies of the New Testament and Beyond* (New York: Crossroad, 1998), p. 227)

What I have tried to share with you is a whole range of pictures, of titles of Jesus, of stories, understandings and descriptions. From the New Testament it is clear that the life, death and resurrection — the whole 'event' of Jesus of Nazareth — produced a great mushrooming of theological speculation, debate, and analysis about what Jesus has done and who Jesus was — or is, now — and then.

Unity and Diversity

One of the things we noted in Chapter 3 about the plurality of the four Gospels is that they contain different portraits, but of one and the same person: they tell the same story of the preacher who taught and healed, was rejected, suffered and died and then rose again. There are not four Jesuses, but one. Equally, in the rest of the New Testament, from the pen of Paul and others, we have seen a variety of theological understandings of Jesus as each writer tries to explain Jesus and his significance for his readers. Yet behind the different emphases there is still one faith: common to them all in the truth that God has acted decisively, uniquely and supremely in the person of Jesus of Nazareth.

The New Testament does not try to spell that out systematically and theologically. In the following chapters we will see how the early Christian Church set about the job of deciding which of the contemporary ideas about Jesus were acceptable and which were not. These debates led to the classic formulations about the Trinity and Jesus' divine and human natures in the Councils of Nicaea and Chalcedon, which placed some limits on the plurality of possible pictures, and did so in words and concepts appropriate to that era.

For each generation and each individual, however, the Christological question 'Who was Jesus — then?' remains, and leads to the further question 'Who is Jesus — now, to me?'

THE EARLY CHURCH

THE EARLY CHURCH

The Early Church and the
Teaching of Jesus

The next three chapters will look at the response of the early Church to Jesus in the centuries after the writing of the New Testament. The earliest Christians came to believe that Jesus was divine on the basis of their experience of him as Lord, raised to life by God and given a place at God's right hand in heaven; they also came to see his divinity reflected in his earthly life of miracles and teaching. During the first four centuries of the Church, interpretations of the relationship between Jesus as human and Jesus as God became progressively more elaborate, leading eventually to the decisions of the Councils of Nicaea and Chalcedon. This process of doctrinal development will be the subject of Chapter 8.

But it is important to see formal doctrinal statements such as those of the Nicaea and Chalcedon in their wider religious and theological context; in this chapter, we will look at how the early Church responded to the moral teaching of Jesus, and in the next at the place of Jesus in early Christian worship. In both we will focus on the evidence of writings of the first three centuries, the formative period of Christian theology; fourth- and fifth-century authors will figure more largely in Chapter 8.

The Importance of the Early Church

Until well after the sixteenth-century Reformation, both the doctrinal statements of Church councils such as Nicaea and Chalcedon and the teaching of the leading theologians of the early Church (the Church fathers) occupied a privileged place in Christian theology. For Eastern Orthodox and Roman Catholic theologians, it was an axiom of faith that the doctrine of the Church fathers and councils ('tradition' as opposed to Scripture) must be preserved unchanged. For Protestants, although supreme authority in matters of faith lay with the Bible and nothing was required to be believed which it did not explicitly teach, the writings of the Church fathers were nonetheless often seen as a true guide to the way in which the Bible ought to be interpreted to ensure the identity of the beliefs and practices of the Church of the present day (including its system of government and its worship as well as its theology) with those of Christians of the apostolic age.

Although, as we have seen in Chapter 1, some more recent theologians have rejected the notion that Christians are obliged to believe in the doctrines of the early Church in exactly the terms in which they were first formulated, few have rejected the theological ideas of the early Church entirely. Modern theologians of all traditions are more aware than their predecessors of the philosophical and cultural factors which affected the ways in which early theologians articulated their faith, and less inclined to see the expression of the faith in terms of Greco-Roman philosophical ideas as authoritative for all time. But even so, many would agree that the Church fathers, as Christians working out their faith in the context of the Church's life and worship, had, if not an authoritative understanding of the original meaning of the Christian faith as expressed in the New Testament, at least a very valuable one, because of their closeness in time and culture to the New Testament itself and because the early Church preserved, in its preaching, worship, and theological reflection, a collective memory of the life and teaching of Jesus and the apostles. The Church fathers must have some importance for contemporary Christians, simply because they were the first to respond to the New Testament message with creative theological ideas. So a great deal of modern theology, whether its focus is worship, prayer, ministry, church life, or Christian ethics, still takes its inspiration and its starting point from the early Church.

The Writings of the Church Fathers

The writings of the Church fathers span not only four or five centuries in time but also a huge geographical area, from Palestine, Syria, and Egypt in the eastern Mediterranean to Italy, Gaul (modern France), and North Africa in the west. When beginning to study their theology it is important to remember that, though all Christians prayed and worshipped and responded to the New Testament message about Jesus in their personal lives, only a small number articulated their faith in writing, and, of these, only a small proportion of early Christian writings have survived to the present day. We need to read the writings of the Church fathers in the awareness that the picture we have is only a partial one. Much remains uncertain about the early Church, in both history and theology, and inevitably modern theologians will sometimes disagree about the interpretation of the theology of the early Church both in its own context and in relation to its significance for today. Nevertheless, the role which the writings of the Church fathers and the doctrinal statements of the councils of the early Church continue to occupy in modern theological thought is sufficient justification for devoting a good deal of space to them.

Jesus' Teaching in Early Christian Thought

Why look first at what the early Church made of the moral teaching of Jesus? The answer is mainly to redress the balance. While it would be untrue to say that the teaching of Jesus was neglected by theologians of the early Church, it received less attention than it might have done. The greatest efforts of early Christian theologians were devoted to establishing that Jesus was divine, or that he fulfilled Old Testament prophecies of a coming Jewish Messiah — a concern already obvious in the New Testament. As a consequence, modern study of the early Church's understanding of Jesus has tended to focus mainly on the development of the Church's distinctive doctrines about him. But, as already noted, it is important to consider the wider theological context in which doctrines about Jesus were set. In considering early Christian responses to the moral teaching of Jesus, we will learn a good deal about the nature of early Christian theology and about the early Church as a religious movement.

Some Theologians of the Early Church

Ignatius: Bishop of Antioch in Syria. Known through seven surviving letters written to churches in Asia Minor (modern Turkey). Arrested, taken to Rome, and executed as a Christian in the second decade of the second century CE.

Justin Martyr: a Christian teacher who before his conversion had been an adherent of Platonist philosophy. Born in Samaria, he later lived in Rome. The author of two important *Apologies* or defences of Christianity. Died between 162 and 167.

Irenaeus: Bishop of Lyons in Gaul, though born and educated in Asia Minor. The most important anti-heretical writer of the second century. Died c. 200.

Clement: a Christian teacher in Alexandria (the capital of Roman Egypt). An important apologist and proponent of the employment of philosophical ideas in Christian theology. A contemporary of Irenaeus.

Tertullian: born and lived in Carthage (in modern Tunisia). Probably, like Justin and Clement, a layman. The first theologian to write in Latin. Died c. 220.

Origen: born in Alexandria, c. 184-85. Taught theology in Alexandria and (from c. 231) in Caesarea in Palestine where he was ordained priest. The leading theologian of the time before the Council of Nicaea. Died c. 254. Posthumously

---

The Modern Context of Our Investigation

Jesus' moral teaching is the heart of the gospel message for many modern Christians, especially where poverty and injustice are perceived as the most important moral and social issues facing human beings. God's love for all human beings, the responsibility of human beings for one another, and the primacy of God's peace and justice over human political and social values and institutions are Christian beliefs derived from Je-

116

399) condemned as a heretic by the Bishops of Alexandria and Rome.

Arius: Alexandrian priest and theologian. His teaching provoked the controversy over the doctrine of the Trinity which led to the Council of Nicaea in 325. Died 336.

Athanasius: Bishop of Alexandria 328-73 (though exiled five times by his opponents). Defender of the Council of Nicaea. The most important theologian of the fourth century.

Basil of Caesarea: Bishop of Caesarea in Cappadocia (eastern Turkey) from 370. Important founder of Christian monastic communities. Defender of Nicaea and supporter of Athanasius. Died 377 or 379.

Gregory of Nyssa: Basil's younger brother and like him a defender of Nicaea. Died c. 395.

Gregory of Nazianzus: friend of Basil and Gregory of Nyssa. Particularly important as a defender of the divinity of the Holy Spirit. Together the three friends are referred to as the Cappadocian Fathers. Died c. 389.

Cyril of Alexandria: Bishop of Alexandria 412-44. Opposed the teaching of **Nestorius** (Bishop of Constantinople 428-31; died c. 450) about the person of Jesus. The controversy between the two led ultimately to the Council of Chalcedon in 451 and the formal statement of the doctrine of the incarnation.

sus' moral teaching — and of course from the example of his life of compassion and service offered freely on behalf of his fellow human beings.

Modern Christians have also used Jesus' moral teaching as a basis from which to identify common ground between Christians and other moral viewpoints, whether religious teachings, secular philosophies, or political ideas. For example, common ground may be identified between the pacifist strand in Christianity (derived from Jesus' teaching on responding to evil with love) and Buddhism or Hinduism, religions whose moral values have generally included non-violence and tolerance. Other links have been made between Christianity and movements of liberation such as Marxism and feminism, study of which has encouraged many Christians to commit themselves more fully to making Jesus' opposition to injustice, poverty, and violence an effective political force in the modern world.

The desire to build bridges between Christianity and other world religions and to see Christian moral teaching on injustice and poverty as allied with (and thus able to learn from) secular and religious systems of thought which have similar social and political goals is something which is distinctive of modern Christianity, particularly since the twentieth century, in which secular ideologies flourished and Western societies became more aware than before of alternative religious and social systems to their own. Early Christians would have agreed that injustice and poverty are important issues, but we should not expect them to share the outlook of modern Christians. They had polemical and apologetic concerns of their own, related to their own religious and social context and outlook, and we need to understand some of these in order to see why their emphases in relation to the moral teaching of Jesus were different from those typical of many Christians today.

Apology/apologetic: a type of speech or writing devoted to defence of a religious belief, often by showing that it is more reasonable or morally superior to opposing positions. An important genre of Christian literature in the second and third centuries CE.

Contexts of Early Christian Moral Teaching

The Debate with Judaism

Throughout the centuries of the early Church, but particularly in the first and second centuries CE, Christians were concerned with asserting their identity in relation to Judaism, the religion from which Christianity had emerged. Their distinctive beliefs, and therefore the source of conflict with Judaism, centred on their view of Jesus' status as Messiah,

Son of God, and Saviour, not on moral issues, about which Jews and Christians generally shared the same assumptions. As conflict with Judaism did not centre on moral issues, it did not encourage Christians to stress the distinctiveness of Jesus' teaching over against that of their parent religion. This is one reason why the teaching of Jesus can sometimes appear to be of less interest to early Christians than the doctrine of his divinity.

The moral assumptions which Jews and Christians shared were based on the Ten Commandments and, more generally, on the moral teaching of the Old Testament Law and prophets, and this in broad outline is very largely what is reflected in the teaching of Jesus. Jesus was not the first religious teacher within Judaism to oppose injustice, violence, and poverty, to call for repentance for sins, to say that love was more important than religious ritual, or to teach the importance of sexual morality, including fidelity in marriage and the avoidance of lust and adultery. In that sense, Christians generally shared the moral framework of Judaism, and could describe their moral life largely in terms drawn from the Old Testament, as for example in Justin's *Dialogue with Trypho*, an account of a discussion between Justin and a Jewish teacher:

> And we who were filled full of war, and slaughter of one another, and every kind of evil, have from out of the whole earth each changed our weapons of war, our swords into ploughshares and our pikes into farming tools, and we farm piety, righteousness, and love of man, faith, and hope which comes from the Father himself through him who was crucified. (Section 110; *New Eusebius*, p. 59, referring to Isaiah 2.4/Micah 4.3)

The one big exception to this generalization about shared moral assumptions was that early Christians argued with Jews about the extent to which they were bound by the specifically religious or ritual aspects of the Old Testament Law. Early Christians on the whole believed that Jesus had taught that it was not necessary for his followers to continue to obey the Law. They would cite examples from the Gospels where Jesus had said, for example, that the Jewish food laws or laws about ritual purity were unimportant, or where Jesus was shown to have broken the laws about keeping the Sabbath.

Jesus' Attitude to the Law

Matthew 5.21, 22	Murder
Matthew 5.27, 28	Adultery
Matthew 5.31, 32	Divorce
Matthew 5.38-44	Revenge
Matthew 12.1-12	Keeping the Sabbath
Matthew 15.1-20	Ritual washing

Modern New Testament scholars have been able to show that on the whole Jesus was not as hostile to the Old Testament Law as early Christians tended to believe. He may have wished to interpret the Old Testament Law in a particular way, to intensify some of its provisions (see the examples in the box), perhaps to accept occasions when it should be broken or when people should be exempted from obedience to it, but he did not wish to see it abandoned.

These modern insights would have been very unfamiliar to the early Christians. They took at face value what they read in the Gospels about Jesus' apparent hostility to the Law, and this was one point in the debate with Judaism where Christians argued a good deal about what Jesus had actually taught (or at least what they thought Jesus had taught), and showed themselves very hostile to the Jewish way of life. Ignatius of Antioch put it very simply: 'if we live according to Judaism, we confess that we have not received grace' (*Magnesians*, 8; *New Eusebius*, pp. 13-14); and he went on to contrast 'keeping the Sabbath' — i.e. Judaism — with 'a life ruled by the Lord's day' — i.e. the resurrection, therefore the life of Christians.

The Debate with Paganism

Much of the intellectual energy of second-century Christianity was taken up with apologetic debate with Greco-Roman paganism. On the whole the line taken by Christians in this debate was that Christianity taught a superior monotheism to pagan religion, that is a doctrine of one true God, the creator of all things. Christians regarded paganism as the worship of idols or demons, and devoted much of their energy to attacking it. Though they were well aware that pagan religion had been criticized by some of the Greek philosophers, poets, and dramatists, and were quick to claim these as evidence for the truth of what Christians taught, nevertheless, from a Christian point of view, it was only Christianity that had come to grasp the doctrine of the one true God in all its fullness.

Because Christians rejected the worship of the gods of paganism, they were considered atheists by many pagan critics and liable to punishment by the Roman authorities, so it was essential for them to prove that they worshipped the true God, and that Jesus was his incarnate Son (see,for example, Justin, *First Apology*, 5-6; *New Eusebius*, p. 60). Historical and philosophical evidence for of the truth of the Bible and Christian beliefs was adduced in the form of proof that Jesus had been foretold by the Old Testament prophets (thus confirming the divine inspiration of the Jewish Scriptures) and that Christian doctrines were concordant with reason and with the best that could be found in those parts of pagan religious and philosophical teaching that pointed in a monotheistic direction (cf. again Justin, *Second Apology*, 13; *New Eusebius*, pp. 61-62).

The debate with paganism was an important context in which Christians reflected on the moral teaching of their religion. On the whole, early Christian apologists were more concerned to attack pagan religion and to prove the philosophical and historical truth of Christianity than they were to comment on the moral condition of the society they lived in. But there are many places in early Christian writing where the lifestyle of Christians is portrayed as superior to that of pagans — as implicitly, for example, in Justin's comments which were quoted above on the moral condition of people before conversion to Christianity. Later in this chapter we will look in more detail at Justin's apologetic use of Jesus' moral teaching, and at that of his most important successor as an apologist for Christianity in the period we are considering, Origen.

The Social Morality of the Christian Community

Christianity began in rural Palestine and in the city of Jerusalem. It may well have had a revolutionary, or at least a radical, social and moral programme in its beginnings, and this is, as we have seen, an aspect of

Christian moral teaching which many modern Christians wish to stress. But Christianity, like many religious cults, rapidly grew into an urban, middle-class, and essentially socially conservative movement. Typical second- and third-century Christians were by no means wealthy, or leaders of society, but many were reasonably well educated, ordinary, middle-class urban people who were concerned, on the whole, to show that a socially conservative morality — honesty, the family, sexual probity and so on — was a feature of Christianity. This is not by any means to say that such Christians did not reflect on moral issues, that they did not try to follow Jesus' moral teachings, or that their descriptions of their lifestyle are not morally very demanding (see, for example, the glowing portrayal of Christian morality in the *Apology* of Aristides; *New Eusebius*, pp. 52-54). But there is an evident concern to make it clear that Christians fitted into ordinary society, and were not a threat to it. An anonymous Christian apologist, the author of a document called the *Letter to Diognetus*, wrote:

> For Christians are not distinguished from the rest of mankind by country, or by speech, or by dress [. . .] But while they dwell in Greek or barbarian cities according as each man's lot has been cast, and follow the customs of the land in clothing and food, and other matters of daily life, yet the condition of citizenship which they exhibit is wonderful, and admittedly strange. They live in countries of their own, but simply as sojourners; they share the life of citizens, they endure the lot of foreigners; every foreign land is to them a fatherland, and every fatherland a foreign land. (Section 5; *New Eusebius*, p. 55)

Christians, in other words, focus their aspirations on heaven rather than earth and do not form a distinct political — and therefore potentially rebellious — community (as Judaism had done before the defeat of the Jewish rebellions against the Roman empire of 66-70 and 132-35 CE). This can give the impression, to modern Christians, that early Christians' appreciation of the radical character of Jesus' moral teaching was not very great; but perhaps, given the fact that Christians were a tiny minority in the Greco-Roman world of the second century, and often subject to the threat of persecution because of their perceived atheism (see above), it would be unrealistic to expect them to desire to transform the society in which they lived by political or social action.

The Morality of Christian Intellectuals

Christian intellectuals of the second and third centuries — people like Justin, Clement of Alexandria, and Origen — wrote the earliest works on Christian prayer and spirituality, or personal religious life, as well as theology and apologetic. Christian apologists would happily assert the superiority of Christian moral teaching to paganism, but the same Christian intellectuals who made this point often shared some of the moral assumptions of Greco-Roman philosophers, who tended to view morality and ethics in terms of following out a 'philosophical' lifestyle of personal moral effort and achievement. Moral life was a form of training, of progress towards a condition of stable or habitual goodness, mental tranquillity, and happiness. For Christians, the goal would include enjoyment of a personal relationship with God, perhaps understood in terms of union or contemplation — terms which feature largely in later Christian mystical theology (of which Clement and Origen are two of the founders). Particularly for Clement and Origen, morality also necessarily involved asceticism, which was seen as conducive to a proper devotion to God.

Asceticism: the practice of a disciplined life, usually including strict control of speech, diet, sleep, and sexual desire. From Greek *askesis* ('training').

Mystical theology/mysticism: the branch of theology which deals with how human beings attain a sense of communion, union, or friendship with God, usually through the disciplines of study, prayer, ascetic life, and moral endeavour.

This way of thinking about ethics as part of a programme of personal development, something for which a theologian trained himself over the course of a life of philosophical study and asceticism, means that the focus of early Christian moral writing often falls on the motives for which people want to live a good life, or the character of the just or good man, rather than on, say, obedience to God's or Jesus' commands as a moral or religious duty. Christian moralists were often better at talking about motive and character than they were about the morality of particular actions. Clement, for example, expressed the goal of Christian morality in terms of 'passionlessness' or detachment, in which goodness is practised not for the sake of reputation or heavenly reward but simply out of a desire to live according to the image and likeness of God (cf. Gen. 1.26):

> He, then, who has first moderated his passions and trained himself for impassibility [. . .] is here equal to the angels. Luminous already, and like the sun shining in the exercise of beneficence, he speeds by righteous knowledge through the love of God to the sacred abode, like as the apostles. (*Miscellanies*, book 6; *New Eusebius*, p. 185)

While it would be unfair to say that Christian theologians who thought in these terms ignored the specific moral teaching of Jesus, it is easy to see how in authors influenced by this way of thinking about the moral life, Jesus' concerns for social morality or justice could become subordinated to a more personal, spiritual goal.

Martyrdom and Imitation of Jesus

The social morality of the *Letter to Diognetus* and the intellectual asceticism of Clement and Origen are not, of course, the whole picture when it comes to describing early Christian lifestyles. The general belief of early Christians was that the highest expression of Christian devotion to God was to suffer martyrdom — to confess one's faith before the Roman authorities and, refusing to renounce Christianity, to be put to death.

Willingness to suffer martyrdom expressed not only loyalty to the truth of Christian teaching about God in the face of the temptation to save one's life by agreeing to worship the pagan gods, but also a sense of personal identification with Jesus in his suffering and death. During the second century several accounts of the martyrdom of prominent Christian leaders were written and circulated among the churches as examples to admire and imitate — for example the account of Polycarp, Bishop of Smyrna (*New Eusebius*, pp. 23-30). But belief in the value of martyrdom as a way of responding to Jesus' example of endurance of suffering and as a goal for all Christians who wanted to improve the quality of their discipleship is best exemplified by a comment made by

Ignatius of Antioch who, while under arrest and on the way to Rome to be tried as a Christian, wrote to the Christians of Rome asking them not to attempt to save him from being put to death:

> I am truly in earnest about dying for God — if only you yourselves put no obstacles in the way. I must implore you to do me no such untimely kindness; pray leave me to be a meal for the beasts, for it is they who can provide my way to God. I am his wheat, ground fine by the lions' teeth to be made purest bread for Christ [. . .] When there is no trace of my body left for the world to see, then I shall truly be Jesus Christ's disciple. So intercede with him for me, that by their instrumentality I may be made a sacrifice to God. (Ignatius, *Romans*, 4; translated by M. Staniforth and A. Louth, *Early Christian Writings* [Penguin Classics; Harmondsworth, 1987], p. 86; see also the extract in *New Eusebius*, pp. 12-13)

Any account of what early Christians believed, whether about theological or moral questions, during the three centuries before the conversion of the Emperor Constantine to Christianity in 312 must take into account the possibility which they faced of being persecuted and made to suffer for their faith.

The Use of Jesus' Teaching in Apologetic and Preaching: Justin, Origen and 2 *Clement*

The final section of this chapter will illustrate the use of Jesus' moral teaching by the early Church in more detail. First, we will look at the area of apologetic, which as our survey of some of the contexts of Christian moral teaching has shown, is one of the most promising areas to examine. Justin and Origen are the best examples of apologists who emphasized the superiority of Christian to pagan moral teaching. Finally, we will look at the use of Jesus' moral teaching in a example of early Christian preaching, since preaching was probably the main means by which ordinary Christians in the early Church became acquainted with Jesus' teaching and therefore with what sort of moral commitment was expected of them. We will take as an example an early Christian sermon which goes under the name of 2 *Clement*.

Justin

Justin devotes a few pages of his *First Apology*, addressed to the Roman emperor Antoninus Pius (138-61), to the moral power of Christianity. It is interesting to note that these pages follow directly after the introductory part of the *Apology*, in which Justin refutes the pagan charges that Christians are atheists or that they seek to subvert society or the Roman empire by their behaviour. Thus, Justin offers his remarks on ethics (sections 14-17 of the *First Apology*) as a useful preliminary to discussing in more detail Christian teaching about the person of Jesus and his fulfilment of Old Testament prophecies.

He begins by appealing (as in the passage from the *Dialogue with Trypho* quoted earlier) to the change of lifestyle adopted by those who have ceased to be deceived by the demons who mislead pagan critics of Christianity, and have been persuaded by the Word (i.e., God's Son, Jesus, speaking through Scripture) to 'follow the only unbegotten God' (14).

> Those who formerly delighted in fornication now embrace chastity alone; those who formerly made use of magical arts have dedicated themselves to the good and unbegotten God; we who once valued above everything the gaining of wealth and possessions now bring what we have into a common stock and share with everyone in need; we who hated and destroyed one another, and would not share the same hearth with people of a different tribe on account of their different customs, now since the coming of Christ, live familiarly with them, and pray for our enemies, and try to persuade those who unjustly hate us to live according to the good advice of Christ to the end that they may share with us the same joyful hope of a reward from God the Master of all. (14)

Justin then goes on to invite the addressees of the *Apology*, the emperor and his sons, to examine Christian moral teaching, 'to find out whether we have been taught to do and teach these things truly'. And he makes a pointed contrast between Jesus' moral teaching and the less memorable and accessible teachings of philosophy: 'Short and concise utterances come from him, for he was no sophist, but his word was the power of God.'

> **Sophist**: a term originating in ancient Athens for someone who made a living by teaching techniques of philosophical argument, often specializing in ethics. Often used unfavourably by Christian authors.

The next few paragraphs quote numerous sayings of Jesus, mainly from the Sermon on the Mount (Matt. 5–7), beginning with what Jesus had to say about sexual morality and divorce and moving on to repentance, love of enemies, and giving freely to others (15). Justin then discusses non-resistance to evil and the need for Christians actually to follow Jesus' moral teaching, not merely profess faith in him, in order to be saved (16); finally he mentions Christian willingness, following Jesus' command, to pay taxes and be loyal to the empire, even though they will worship God alone (17).

Justin wants to underline in both individual and communal terms the capacity of Christianity to change people's lives and of Christians to win converts by means of their behaviour as well as to convince the Roman authorities of their harmlessness and indeed value to society. He cites examples of Christian living and its effects on pagans:

Many, both men and women, who have been Christ's disciples since childhood, have preserved their purity at the age of sixty or seventy years; and I am proud that I could produce such from every race of men and women. (15)

Many who were once of your way of thinking [. . .] have turned from the way of violence and tyranny, being conquered, either by the constancy of life which they have traced in [Christian] neighbors, or by the strange endurance which they have noticed in defrauded fellow travelers or have experienced in those with whom they had dealings. (16)

Justin is so convinced of the power of Christian moral teaching that he challenges the emperor to act against Christians who fail to live up to it: 'as to those who are not living in accordance with his teachings, but are Christians only in name, we demand that all such shall be punished by you' (16). Though he must have known of Christians whose morality was lax, Justin would not have made this remark if he had believed that failure to obey Jesus' moral teaching was characteristic of the Christian community in general.

These sections of Justin's *First Apology* are among the longest surviving passages of quotation from Jesus' moral teaching to have been penned by a second-century Christian author. Justin may sound a bit naïve in his linking together of so many of Jesus' sayings without a great deal of exposition or comment, but his is one of the first attempts to talk to a pagan audience about what was involved in being converted to Christianity and living out a Christian life in a pagan world. Justin, who had studied philosophy and appreciated its value in preparing the way for Christian monotheistic beliefs, is nevertheless not afraid to point out those areas in which he believes the teaching of Jesus is superior to, and stronger than, the ethics of pagan philosophy or religion.

As he says later in the *First Apology*, when he is talking about baptism, baptism is for 'as many as are persuaded and believe that the things we teach and say are true, and undertake to live accordingly' (61). 'Persuaded' is an important word for Justin, and he clearly places the moral teaching of Jesus and the example of the Christian community at the forefront of the evidence that he hopes will convince pagans of the truth of what Christians teach.

Origen

Origen was the most remarkable and also the most controversial figure in third-century Christianity. He was a biblical commentator, preacher, apologist, and writer of systematic and philosophical treatises about Christian doctrine. He was one of the few Gentile Christians in antiquity who took the trouble to learn Hebrew in order to read the Old Testament in its original language (and also to talk to Jewish rabbis about the interpretation of Scripture). His ascetic understanding of Christian life and his mystical interpretations of Scripture laid the foundations for the Christian monastic movement, which began in Egypt not long after Origen's death and was probably influenced by his writings. At the end of the fourth century Origen was condemned as a heretic because of several controversial features of his theology, particularly his belief in the pre-existence of souls and his universalism, which may have included the belief that even the devil could repent of his sins and be saved.

> **Pre-existence of souls**: the doctrine, derived from Plato (427-347 BCE), that human souls exist in a spiritual world before they are incarnated in bodies.
>
> **Universalism**: the belief that all human beings will be saved. Typically, universalists such as Origen believe that hell is not a permanent state of punishment, even for the most wicked human beings, but a place in which they are encouraged by God to repent of their sins and undergo moral re-education or purification.

As an apologist, Origen in many ways picks up where Justin left off, developing Justin's reasoned defence of Christian teaching and appeal to philosophical support for Christian monotheism. But as regards his use of the teaching of Jesus, Origen's apologetic has an interesting feature which Justin's lacks, in that Origen was aware of pagan attacks on the Bible, including on Jesus' teaching.

This is seen in his apologetic work, *Against Celsus,* in which Origen replied to a second-century pagan philosopher who had studied the Bible and observed the arguments used by Christians in their defence of Jesus' divine status. (Origen composed *Against Celsus* in the 240s, about seventy years after Celsus' critique of Christianity, the *True Word,* had been written. Celsus' work is known only through the quotations in Origen's reply.)

Celsus was not convinced of the uniqueness, as God's incarnate Son, which Christians ascribed to Jesus, and pertinently asked why Christians, if they regarded Old Testament prophecies and the New Testament accounts of Jesus' miracles as proofs of his divinity, did not accept similar arguments in favour of the truth of the stories told about some of the pagan gods (see *Against Celsus,* 2.55 and 7.3). Celsus also uses other arguments against Jesus' divinity, for example that Jesus, if he is God, should provide evidence of this by protecting his followers from persecution (8.39). Much of Origen's *Against Celsus* is taken up with replies to Celsus' arguments of this sort.

Celsus' attempt to relativize Jesus by showing that there is nothing special about him compared with paganism extends to his treatment of Jesus' moral teaching. In two interesting passages, Celsus argues that Jesus' teaching is really just an inferior version of philosophical teaching to be found in Plato. Jesus told his followers that it is easier for a camel to pass through the eye of a needle than for a rich person to enter the Kingdom of Heaven (Matt. 19.24). But Plato had said that it was impossible to be distinguished for both riches and goodness (*Against Celsus*, 6.16). Similarly, Jesus' command not to resist evil but to 'turn the other cheek' (Matt. 5.39) is a cruder version of Plato's argument against repaying one act of injustice with another (7.58).

Origen's reply to these arguments against the special value of Jesus' moral teaching points to where he thinks the superiority of Christianity over pagan philosophy actually lies. In the first instance, he pours scorn on the idea that Jesus could have read Plato and simply decided to rephrase Plato's teaching on riches in a peculiar way. Jesus chose the illustration of the camel, Origen says, because camels are 'unclean' beasts according to the Jewish Law. In other words, we might say (for Origen himself does not carry the argument through), Jesus' choice of image was appropriate to the mindset of his Jewish hearers, and would have suggested, by the very use of an 'unclean' animal as an example, the morally tainted character of riches. Origen goes on to say, however, that the unexpected choice of image should prompt the reader to examine Jesus' other pronouncements of blessing on the poor and woe to the rich (Matt. 5.3; Luke 6.20, 24), to see whether or not they are meant to be taken absolutely literally. If they are not — he implies — then Jesus must have been referring to a more spiritual quality, not to material wealth or poverty. It is typical of Origen's method of interpreting the Bible to use apparently incongruous statements or images, such as a camel passing through of the eye of a needle, to justify the search for a meaning beyond the literal sense of what Scripture says.

In the second case, non-resistance to evil, Origen produces a more straightforward response to Celsus' criticism, arguing that Jesus' saying is not a cruder version of Plato's argument, as Celsus thought, but on the contrary a more beneficial one because it can be understood by ordinary people — whereas even philosophers have difficulty in understanding Plato (7.61).

The argument here is similar to, though more explicit than, Justin's comment that Jesus' moral sayings are 'short and concise', and not the philosophical teachings of a sophist. For both Justin and Origen, Jesus' teaching was the clearest point of God's revelation to human beings, and that of course was because Jesus was the divine word *(logos)* or communication, living as a human being.

Origen, then, is aware of the need to defend the teaching of Jesus. Unlike Justin, he does not just put it forward as obviously superior to what pagans think about moral issues. Nevertheless, like Justin, he sees Jesus' moral teaching as proved true by its power as a force for the conversion of human beings. But the moral force of the teaching of Jesus was in turn rooted in the quality of his own life; that Jesus taught both his disciples and other hearers how to live in accordance with God's will is what Origen uses to prove (in response to another line of criticism from Celsus) that Jesus was a good man and therefore no mere practitioner of sorcery, but a worker of real miracles, and indeed God:

> Is it not likely that one who used the miracles that he performed to call those who saw the happenings to moral reformation, would have shown himself as an example of the best life, not only to his genuine disciples but also to the rest? Jesus did this in order that his disciples might give themselves to teaching men according to the will of God, and that the others, who have been taught as much by his teaching as by his moral life and miracles the right way to live, might do every action by referring to the pleasure of the supreme God. If the life of Jesus was of this character, how could anyone [i.e. Celsus] reasonably compare him with the behaviour of sorcerers and fail to believe that according to God's promise he was God who had appeared in a human body for the benefit of our race? (1.68; *New Eusebius*, pp. 208-9)

2 Clement

Very few sermons survive from the first two centuries of Christianity. One of the most interesting is known as 2 *Clement,* or the *Second letter of Clement,* because it came to be attributed to Clement of Rome, one of the earliest Roman bishops, who died in the late first century. In fact it is anonymous and its date is uncertain, though it can probably be placed in the second century.

2 *Clement* is one of the earliest Christian writings to quote extensively from Jesus' teaching. The author uses both the Gospels and also some non-canonical sayings of Jesus — that is, sayings which are quoted by writers in the early Church, probably on the basis of oral tradition, but which never found their way into the Gospel texts. What we find in this sermon is quite a careful working out, by an able preacher, of what Christians need to do in order to be saved and enter the Kingdom of God, based on what Jesus said. For example:

> Let us wait, therefore, hour by hour, for the kingdom of God in love and righteousness, since we do not know the day of God's appearing. For the Lord himself, when he was asked by someone when his kingdom was going to come, said, 'When the two shall be one, and the outside like the inside, and the male with the female, neither male nor female'. Now 'the two' are 'one' when we speak the truth among ourselves and there is one soul in two bodies without deception. And by 'the outside like the inside', he means this: the 'inside' signifies the soul, while the 'outside' signifies the body. Therefore just as your body is visible, so also let your soul be evident in good works. And by 'the male with the female, neither male nor female' he means this: that when a brother sees a sister, he should not think of her as female, nor should she think of him as male. When you do these things, he says, the kingdom of my Father will come. (Section 12)

To appreciate this it does not matter that the saying of Jesus quoted is a non-canonical one. Although the author of the sermon quotes from the Gospels (Matt. 9.13) as 'Scripture' (section 2), and therefore knew of the Gospels as written texts, he also regarded this non-canonical saying, from whatever oral or written source he drew it, as authoritative. Maybe, from a modern point of view, having an unfamiliar saying of Jesus to think about helps to highlight the way in which the author deliberately uses the quotation, expounding its moral implications in good sermonic style, and thus showing what sort of obedience is required of Christians if they are to enter the Kingdom.

In another passage, a contrast between this age and the age to come, to which Christians look forward, is drawn out of two juxtaposed sayings of Jesus (Matt. 6.24 and 16.26):

> Now the Lord says, 'No servant can serve two masters'. If we wish to serve both God and money, it is harmful to us. 'For what good is it, if someone gains the whole world but forfeits his life?' This age and the one that is coming are two enemies. This one talks about adultery and corruption and greed and deceit, but that one renounces these things. We cannot, therefore, be friends of both; we must renounce this one in order to experience that one. We think that it is better to hate what is here, because it is insignificant and transitory and perishable, and to love what is there, things which are good and imperishable. For if we do the will of Christ we will find rest; but if we do not, if we disobey his commandments, then nothing will save us from eternal punishment. (Section 6)

This is an example of what must have been done by many Christian preachers in sermons — perhaps especially when expounding Jesus' parables or other enigmatic sayings — and it reminds us of what sort of knowledge and understanding of Jesus' teaching probably underlies the more formal apologetic and theological writings of the early Church.

Jesus in Early Christian Worship

In the second half of the twentieth century many of the Christian churches reformed their worship, often drawing on the evidence of the early Church in an attempt to recover the original significance of the rites or liturgies which they had inherited from the past. Partly because of the importance of this movement of liturgical renewal in the recent history of the churches, the worship of the early Church has become a focus of intense study, and a topic which no theologian or other student of Christianity can afford to neglect.

> **Rite**: the words said or sung and the actions performed during an act of worship.
>
> **Liturgy**: a term for an act of worship usually implying the following of a fixed form of words or actions rather than an improvised or extempore one. From Greek *leitourgia,* 'service'.

In this chapter we will focus mainly on the liturgies of the two Gospel or dominical sacraments of baptism and the Eucharist (also known as the Lord's Supper or Holy Communion), and with how ideas about Jesus are incorporated in these.

> **Sacrament**: according to the classic definition found in the Church of England's Book of Common Prayer, 'an outward and visible sign of an inward and spiritual grace given to us'.
>
> **Gospel or dominical sacraments**: the two sacraments, baptism and the Eucharist, which Jesus is stated in the Gospels to have instituted and to have commanded his disciples to continue. See Matt. 28.19, Mark 14.22-25, 1 Corinthians 11.23-26. 'Dominical' is from Latin *Dominus* ('Lord').

Introduction to Early Christian Worship

Sources

The New Testament tells us a lot about early Christian worship and the meaning of baptism and the Eucharist, and we shall look at some of this evidence in the course of this chapter. Many of the Church fathers also mention worship and the sacraments in their writings. But there are several early sources which give fuller or more explicit information.

The Didache

One of the earliest of these is a second-century document known as the *Didache,* from the Greek word for 'teaching'. The full title is *The teaching of the Lord to the Gentiles, through the twelve apostles.* The *Didache* is the earliest example of a type of writing known as a 'church order', a set of rules dealing with aspects of church life including worship and the sacraments. The *Didache* embodies material that probably took shape in Palestine or Syria around the year 100, and the whole text is unlikely to be later than 150. Brief though it is, the *Didache* contains one of the earliest descriptions of baptism outside the New Testament, and the earliest set of instructions for worship on Sunday or the Lord's day (see box).

Extracts from the *Didache* (*New Eusebius*, pp. 9-12)

On baptism: Baptize in the Name of the Father, and of the Son and of the Holy Spirit, in running water. But if you have no running water, baptize in other water; and, if you cannot in cold, in warm. But if you have neither, pour water thrice upon the head in the name of Father, Son and Holy Spirit. And before the baptism let the baptizer and him that is baptized fast, and such others as can; and you shall bid the person to be baptized to fast for one or two days before.

(Section 7)

On Sunday worship: Come together and break bread and give thanks [*or*, offer the Eucharist], having first confessed your transgressions, that your sacrifice may be pure. But whoever has a dispute with his fellow, let him not come together with you, until they be reconciled, that your sacrifice be not polluted. For this is what was spoken by the Lord, 'In every place and time offer me a pure sacrifice: for I am a great king saith the Lord, and my name is wonderful among the gentiles'.

(Section 14, quoting Malachi 1.10, 14)

Justin

Justin, who is so important a source for Christian apologetic and theology in the second century, also offers important evidence for worship. His *First Apology*, sections 61-67, describes first the rite of baptism (including the baptismal Eucharist, at which the newly baptized Christian participates in the Eucharist for the first time), then Sunday worship. Justin shows that the Eucharist consisted of readings from Scripture, a sermon, prayers, and the sharing of bread and wine (see box).

The Apostolic Tradition

In third place is another church order, the *Apostolic Tradition*. This text contains a more detailed description of baptism than either the

---

Justin on the Eucharist (*New Eusebius*, pp. 63-64)

[. . .] At the end of the prayers, we salute one another with a kiss. There is then brought to the president of the brethren bread and a cup of wine mixed with water; and he taking them, offers up praise and glory to the Father of the universe, through the name of the Son and of the Holy Spirit, and gives thanks at considerable length for our being counted worthy to receive these things at his hands. When he has concluded the prayers and thanksgivings, all the people present express their joyful assent by saying Amen [. . . Then] those who are called by us deacons give to each of those present to partake of the bread and wine mixed with water over which thanksgiving was pronounced, and to those who are absent they carry away a portion.

(*First Apology*, 65)

Didache or Justin, and instructions for daily prayer. It also includes the first surviving examples of prayers used at ordinations to the three orders of Christian ministry which developed in the early Church — bishops, priests, and deacons. About the Eucharist it supplies similar information to Justin, except that it preserves an example of the sort of prayer which a bishop would use to give thanks (in Greek, *eucharistein*, from which the word 'Eucharist' is derived) over the bread and wine. (This prayer will be quoted and discussed later in this chapter.)

Opinions differ about the date and origin of the *Apostolic Tradition*, but many scholars have placed it in Rome around the year 220, and seen it as the work of Hippolytus, a theologian who may have died as a martyr in c. 235. In the absence of definite evidence to the contrary, this is probably still the safest opinion to hold.

Other Sources

From the later second and third centuries we have evidence from Irenaeus, Tertullian, Bishop Cyprian of Carthage (d. 258), and Origen. From the fourth century, the available evidence becomes much more abundant, but since it is the earliest sources which often provide the most illuminating information for helping us to understand the early Church's response to Jesus, this chapter will confine itself to the evidence of the second- and third-century sources.

Daily Prayer

Before we look at baptism and the Eucharist in the early Church, it is important to recall that the basis of early Christian worship of God was the practice of daily prayer. This was inherited by early Christians from Judaism, but it was not by any means exclusively Jewish. Both private and public prayer would also have been readily understood and frequently practised in a pagan religious environment. Right from the very earliest Christian sources there is evidence that daily prayer was taught by Christian leaders. All Christians were expected to engage in it, including, on occasions, being prepared to get up during the night to pray. They were also encouraged to stop work several times a day to give thanks and to offer their prayers to God.

The *Apostolic Tradition* on Daily Prayer

The faithful, as soon as they have woken and got up, before they go to their work, shall pray to God and then hasten to their work. If there is any instruction in the word, he should give priority to this and go to hear the word of God.

(Section 35; Alistair Stewart-Sykes,
Hippolytus. On the Apostolic Tradition
(New York: St Vladimir's Seminary Press, 2001), p. 156)

The Lord's Prayer

The prayer which Christians know as the Lord's Prayer or the Our Father, taught by Jesus in the Gospels (Matt. 6.9-13; Luke 11.2-4), was clearly at the heart of Christian prayer from an early date. The *Didache* is the first post-New Testament writing to refer to its use, instructing that the Lord's Prayer should be said three times a day (section 8). Later, in the third century, Tertullian, Cyprian, and Origen all wrote commentaries on the Lord's Prayer which reflect its importance.

Tertullian on the Lord's Prayer

In proportion as it is restrained in wording, so it is copious in meaning. For it embraces not merely the particular functions of prayer, be it the worship of God or man's petition, but as it were the whole of the Lord's discourse, the whole record of his instruction: so that without exaggeration, there is comprised in the prayer an epitome of the entire gospel.

(*On the Prayer,* 1; Ernest Evans, *Tertullian's Tract on the Prayer* (London: SPCK, 1953), p. 5)

There is, perhaps unexpectedly, no evidence that at this time the Lord's Prayer formed part of daily public worship, as opposed to private prayer. Regular public worship (other than the Eucharist) would have been based mainly on instruction by a teacher or preacher and on singing of the Psalms from the Old Testament. The Lord's Prayer did not come to be included in the liturgy of the Eucharist until the fourth century.

Baptism

Baptism is a rite of initiation, the process by which converts to Christianity acknowledge their faith in Jesus and come to be accepted into full membership of the Christian community. (This at least is the case with *adult* baptism, which was the usual form in the early Church and to which most of the surviving evidence refers.) As Christians developed liturgies or services for the occasion, baptism came to be seen not simply as an action performed with the candidate as its subject or recipient, but as an act of worship and prayer towards God in its own right.

Complex liturgies of baptism developed, involving a series of prayers with different purposes. Water was used to baptize the candidate either by pouring or by immersion, and oil was often used to anoint the candidate as well, either before or after baptism in water or sometimes — as in the *Apostolic Tradition* — both. Prayers might be said to consecrate the water and oil before they were used, for the candidate him- or herself, and (either before or after the actual baptism) for the effectiveness of what was being done in bringing salvation and spiritual strength to the baptized. Usually these prayers would be said by the presiding minister — who in the early Church would normally be the bishop of the local community; but some of them might be said by other ministers, by the candidate's sponsors (members of the church who testified to the candidate's wish to repent of his or her sins and become a Christian), or by the candidate him- or herself. Prayer might be accompanied by the gesture of laying of hands on the candidate by the bishop (for the New Testament origins of this see Acts 8.17 and 19.6).

The Bishop's Prayer for the Newly Baptized
(Accompanied by Laying On of Hands)

O Lord God, you have made them worthy to obtain remission of sins through the laver of regeneration of the Holy Spirit; send into them your grace, that they may serve you according to your will; for yours is the glory, to the Father and the Son, with the Holy Spirit in the holy church, both now and world without end. Amen.

(*Apostolic Tradition*, 22; *New Eusebius*, p. 143)

In addition to prayer and the use of water and oil, the main component of the liturgy of baptism was a confession of faith by the person being baptized. The brief account of baptism in the *Didache* does not mention this (any more than it does the use of oil, which may not have begun at such an early date), but it is implied by Justin's references to the assent of the candidate to Christian teaching (*First Apology*, 61, 65). In the *Apostolic Tradition* the candidate answers questions put to him or her by the minister while standing in the baptismal water (see box).

The creeds familiar to many Christians today, such as the Apostles' creed and the Nicene creed (called this because the earliest form of it was approved at the Council of Nicaea — see Chapter 8) developed

---

The Baptismal Interrogation

And when he who is being baptized goes down into the water, he who baptizes him, putting his hand on him, shall say thus:
Do you believe in God, the Father Almighty?

And he who is being baptized shall say:
I believe.

Then holding his hand placed on his head, he shall baptize him once. And then he shall say:
Do you believe in Christ Jesus, the Son of God, who was born by the Holy Ghost of the Virgin Mary, and was crucified under Pontius Pilate, and was dead and buried, and rose again the third day, alive from the dead, and ascended into heaven, and sat at the right hand of the Father, and will come to judge the quick and the dead?

And when he says,
I believe,

he is baptized again. And again he shall say:
Do you believe in the Holy Ghost; in the holy Church, and the resurrection of the flesh?

He who is being baptized shall say accordingly:
I believe,

and so he is baptized a third time.

(*Apostolic Tradition*, 21; *New Eusebius*, p. 142)

---

from baptismal confessions of faith of this type. Creeds have a threefold structure, covering beliefs about the Father, the Son, and the Holy Spirit and other articles of faith. As the *Apostolic Tradition* shows, this structure corresponds to the pattern of baptism itself. From the earliest times (see the *Didache*), immersion in or pouring of water would be done three times, corresponding to the three persons of the Trinity.

The Eucharist

As we have seen, the way in which the Eucharist or Holy Communion was celebrated is described by Justin, who supplements the New Testament evidence for Christians meeting to break bread (Acts 2.42; 20.7) or share the Lord's Supper (a term used by Paul in 1 Cor. 11.20), and shows that by the middle of the second century, a formal liturgy or order of service had begun to develop. Holy Communion was no longer part of a meal shared by believers but something separate, believed to have a special status derived from Jesus' words when he instituted the Eucharist on the night before he died (Mark 14.22-25; 1 Cor. 11.23-26), in which he spoke of the bread and wine as his body and blood. Justin quotes Jesus' words of institution explicitly as evidence that the eucharistic bread and wine are no longer ordinary food but Jesus' body and blood (*First Apology*, 66). Paul had already spoken similarly in 1 Corinthians 10.16 ('The cup of blessing that we bless, is it not a sharing in the blood of Christ? The bread that we break, is it not a sharing in the body of Christ?' NRSV), and the author of Luke's Gospel (24.30, 35), when he explains that the disciples who met the risen Jesus on the road to Emmaus recognized him when he broke bread for them to eat, probably also implies that the Eucharist is the place where early Christians encountered Jesus in their worship.

The Eucharistic Prayer

The core of the liturgy of the Eucharist as it developed in the early Church consisted of the prayer of thanksgiving said over the bread and wine by the minister of the Eucharist, followed by the sharing of the bread and wine itself. As in baptism, the minister (the person referred to by Justin as the 'president') would usually be the bishop of the local church. The prayer of thanksgiving is what in modern liturgies is called the eucharistic prayer or the prayer of consecration; another traditional term (used in Catholic theology) is the canon of the mass.

Because Justin does not actually quote the eucharistic prayer — in fact he implies that the 'president' would extemporize it — it is not clear what elements it contained other than the expression of thanks to God which gives it its name. But probably from the third century (as for example, in the *Apostolic Tradition*; see box), Jesus' words of institution came to be incorporated in the eucharistic prayer of many churches. This was a logical step given that the Eucharist derived its meaning from Jesus' actions and words at the Last Supper.

Eucharistic Offering

Other features of later eucharistic prayers (again, found for the first time in the *Apostolic Tradition*) are an expression of *remembrance* (cf. 1 Cor. 11.24-25) of Jesus' death and resurrection, and of *offering* of the bread and wine (or the whole action of the Eucharist) to God. The idea of offering (sometimes referred to as 'oblation') was particularly important, since early Christians saw the whole of their lives as a pure or spiritual offering or sacrifice (cf. Rom. 12.1), in which worship played an important part. The *Didache* (section 14, quoted earlier in this chapter) is not alone in seeing Christian worship in these terms. Irenaeus linked the idea with Christians' gratitude to God — the bread and wine of the Eucharist representing his gifts to human beings in creation, as well as the spiritual gift of eternal life:

> We are bound to make our oblation to God and thus to show ourselves in all things grateful to him as creator [. . .] And it is only the church which offers a pure oblation to the creator, presenting an offering from his creation, with thanksgiving [. . .] We offer to him what is his own, suitably proclaiming the communion and unity of flesh and spirit. For as the bread, which comes from the earth, receives the invocation of God, and then is no longer common bread but eucharist, consists of two things, an earthly and a heavenly, so our bodies, after partaking of the eucharist, are no longer corruptible, having the hope of the eternal resurrection. (*Against Heresies*, 4.18; Bettenson, *Early Christian Fathers*, pp. 95-96)

With the addition of elements like this to the eucharistic prayer (and of other prayers and readings to the Eucharist as a whole), and

---

The Eucharistic Prayer of the *Apostolic Tradition*

The Lord be with you
And with your spirit.
Up with your hearts.
We have them with the Lord.
Let us give thanks to the Lord.
It is fitting and right.

We render thanks to you, O God, through your beloved child Jesus Christ, whom in the last times you sent to us as a savior and redeemer and angel of your will; who is your inseparable Word, through whom you made all things, and in whom you were well pleased. You sent him from heaven into a virgin's womb; he was made flesh and was manifested as your Son, being born of the Holy Spirit and the Virgin. Fulfilling your will and gaining for you a holy people, he stretched out his hands when he should suffer, that he might release from suffering those who have believed in you.

And when he was betrayed to voluntary suffering that he might destroy death, and break the bonds of the devil, and

---

with the development of theological interpretations of the Eucharist such as those of Irenaeus, what had begun as the sharing of a meal of bread and wine by Jesus and his disciples came to be transformed into a complex, carefully thought-out, and theologically significant act of prayer and worship.

Other Aspects of Early Christian Worship

The Liturgical Calendar

Early Christianity inherited from Judaism an annual structure of festivals. These were tied partly to the Jewish experience of redemption, starting with the festival of Passover when the Jews celebrated the Exo-

tread down hell, and shine upon the righteous, and fix a term, and manifest the resurrection, he took bread and gave thanks to you, saying 'Take, eat; this is my body, which shall be broken for you'. Likewise also the cup, saying, 'This is my blood, which is shed for you; when you do this, you make my remembrance'.

Remembering therefore his death and resurrection, we offer to you the bread and the cup, giving you thanks because you have held us worthy to stand before you and minister to you.

And we ask that you would send your Holy Spirit upon the offering of your holy church; that, gathering her into one, you would grant to all who receive the holy things [to receive them] for the fullness of the Holy Spirit for the strengthening of faith in truth; that we may praise and glorify you through your child Jesus Christ; through whom be glory and honor to you, to the Father and Son, with the Holy Spirit, in your holy Church, both now and to the ages of ages. Amen.

(*Apostolic Tradition,* 4; Jasper and Cuming,
Prayers of the Eucharist, p. 35)

dus from Egypt, and partly to the rhythms of the agricultural year in Palestine. This is no surprise: the combination of their perception of their own salvation history — the process by which they had been saved or created by God as a religious community — with the celebration of the natural world and their daily lives was common to many religious groups in antiquity.

Christianity took over the festivals of the Passover and Pentecost directly from Judaism. Passover was the time of the year when Jesus suffered and was raised, so that Easter is the Christian equivalent. The Jewish feast of Pentecost, coming seven weeks after the Passover, was the time which Christians celebrated as marking the start of the public proclamation of Jesus' death and resurrection by the apostles (Acts 2).

These two festivals, Easter and Pentecost, were universally observed by Christians from the first century onwards. They were the core of what became the much more complex liturgical calendar of later centuries. There is some evidence that one of the first dates to be added (perhaps by the late second century) was a commemoration of Jesus' baptism on 6 January — the day now referred to as Epiphany (a word meaning 'manifestation') by Western Christians who, though it is still sometimes connected with Jesus' baptism, usually see it as the anniversary of the visit of the three magi or wise men to the infant Jesus. The celebration of Jesus' birth on 25 December is first attested early in the fourth century, in Rome, from where the observance gradually spread to other churches.

Whereas Christmas and Epiphany are fixed festivals, the correct date of Passover and therefore Easter depends on the date of the first full moon after the spring equinox (in the northern hemisphere). Early in the history of the Church, Christians continued to be dependent on Jewish calculations to determine when this should fall, but from the third century Christian scholars in Rome and Alexandria began to do the necessary astronomical calculations for themselves. The correct dating of Easter was one of the subjects discussed at the Council of Nicaea.

Celebration of the Martyrs

Like most religions, Christianity developed forms of worship connected with funerals and commemoration of the departed. Because of the centrality to Christians of belief in the resurrection of Jesus and the promise of eternal life, they came to place great emphasis on the celebration of the passing into a hoped-for future life of those who had died.

Alongside this went the commemoration of the very special dead — the martyrs who had died for their faith. From the middle of the second century, Christians observed the anniversary of the martyrs' deaths; in a particular church, the annual commemoration of a famous local martyr would become one of the most important days of the liturgical year. This is why we sometimes know the day of the year on which an early martyr died, but not the year itself, about which traditions could become confused (cf. New Eusebius, p. 29, for this problem in relation to the martyrdom of Polycarp).

Celebrations of the feast of the martyr would consist of a communal celebratory meal accompanied by prayers and psalm-singing and perhaps a procession. An account of the martyr's death, known as a *passion,* would be read out. Documents of this type form the basis of later collections of biographies of saints.

Later in the history of the early Church (particularly in the fourth century, when numbers of Christians in the Roman empire were much larger), the festivals of martyrs became popular holidays; they might also become the occasion of fighting between Christians and pagans, or between different Christian groups who regarded one another as heretics.

Church Buildings

In the earliest times Christians worshipped in houses. In other words, members of the Christian community acted as hosts or patrons to a local church, and provided space for use in worship, whether houses they still lived in or houses which were made over solely to church use. Some may have been adapted for worship by the provision of appropriate furniture like a baptistery, or a table or altar for the celebration of the Eucharist, but there were no purpose-built buildings until probably the second half of the third century.

By the beginning of the fourth century church buildings had become common. Most of these would have taken the form of a worship space surrounded by smaller rooms, perhaps where particular members of the community would live, and where equipment (including, by this time, such things as silver lamp stands and other ornaments) or food and clothes to be given to the poor, would be stored. Not until after the conversion of the Emperor Constantine to Christianity in 312 do we find the context of Christian worship becoming much more public, with the adaptation by Christians of the form of building known as a basilica. This consisted of a large rectangular hall with aisles, each side separated from the central space by rows of arches. A large Christian basilica would soon become one of the most prominent buildings of many towns in the Roman empire.

Many other new developments in Christian worship took place in the fourth century, including practices such as pilgrimages to holy places and the cult of the saints and of relics. However, after this general introduction, it is time to move specifically to the place of Jesus in early Christian worship.

Jesus in Early Christian Worship

Prayer to Jesus

Prayer to Jesus is rooted in the earliest Christians' experience of him as risen Lord, and is closely tied up with belief in his divinity. Stephen, traditionally accorded the title of the first Christian martyr, is recorded at the time of his death as having a vision of Jesus in heaven, to whom he was able to pray, 'Lord Jesus, receive my spirit' (Acts 7.59). If this account is historically trustworthy, it may be significant that Paul was present at Stephen's martyrdom, as seeing Stephen respond to the risen Jesus would have given Paul some idea of how to interpret his own vision of Jesus at the time of his conversion (Acts 9.3-6). Stories like this no doubt encouraged early Christians to pray to Jesus, perhaps even to expect him to speak to them in prayer, even if they did not expect to enjoy an actual vision such as occurs in the biblical cases of Stephen and Paul.

Some early theologians objected to this, among them Origen. He argued that though it is proper to address requests and thanksgivings to saints or even ordinary human beings, prayer in the proper sense — a request to God for something which only God can grant, combined with praise — may be addressed only to God the Father (*On Prayer*, 14-16; Bettenson, *Early Christian Fathers*, pp. 236-38). Jesus cannot be the object of such prayers because he himself offered them during his earthly life (Origen, does not, therefore, think that Jesus' resurrection conferred a new status on him in this respect). But at the same time, it is wrong to offer prayer to the Father *apart from* Jesus, for Jesus is the mediator between the Father and human beings, a 'High Priest' who offers Christians' prayers to God. Origen criticizes as foolish Christians who do not realize this and who offer prayers to Jesus. What Christians should expect, Origen thinks, is not just an immediate, personal relationship with Jesus, but a personal (though mediated) relationship with God the Father himself.

Perhaps as a result of criticisms like Origen's, there is not much evidence from the following centuries of early Christianity of prayer directed to Jesus in baptismal and eucharistic liturgies. There are some exceptions, such as the prayer for forgiveness in the eucharistic liturgy, the *Kyrie eleison* (Greek for 'Lord, have mercy'). Perhaps it seems particularly appropriate to pray to Jesus for forgiveness, as it is Jesus who brings the forgiveness of God to Christians; but generally speaking, prayer and worship in the context of the formal liturgy of the Church, used by all Christians, is addressed to God the Father. This does not mean that prayer to Jesus did not continue, but that it was mainly personal and private; for example, prayer to Jesus for help, comfort, or forgiveness was an important part of the monastic movement which had such an important influence on Christian spirituality from the fourth century onwards. An expanded form of the *Kyrie eleison,* typically 'Jesus, Son of God, have mercy on me, a sinner', became one of the most popular prayers in the monastic life of the Eastern Orthodox churches.

Jesus and Baptism

In the early Church various ways in which baptism could be understood were current, all based on important New Testament texts — besides, of course, the basic point that baptism was the means by which sins were forgiven (cf. Acts 2.38).

Christian Baptism and the Baptism of Jesus

The first way is a pattern of baptismal theology modelled on Jesus' own baptism as it is recorded in the four Gospels. When Jesus is baptized by John the Baptist, as he emerges from the water, the Holy Spirit descends on him in the form of a dove, and God says to Jesus, 'You are my Son, my beloved' (Mark and Luke), or to the onlookers, 'This is my Son, my beloved' (Matthew). (In John, it is John the Baptist who bears witness that Jesus is God's chosen one.)

Jesus' Baptism

Matthew 3.13-17

Mark 1.9-11

Luke 3.21-22

John 1.29-34

When an understanding of baptism based on Jesus' own baptism emerges in Christian theology and liturgy, its main elements are that the baptized person receives God's Holy Spirit (this is often associated in liturgy with an anointing with baptismal oil) and is made to share in the relationship of sonship which Jesus enjoyed to the Father. Origen is representative of early Christian thinking, here as often:

> The gift of the Spirit is represented under the figure of oil; so that he who is converted from sin may not only achieve purification but also be filled with the Holy Spirit, whereby he may also receive his former robe and the ring, be reconciled completely to his Father, and restored to the status of a son. (*Homilies on Leviticus*, 8.2; Bettenson, *Early Christian Fathers*, p. 247)

(Origen's reference to the robe and ring alludes to Jesus' parable of the prodigal son (Luke 15.11-32), where a robe and a ring are given by the father to his wayward son when he returns.)

Later in the Gospels (Matt. 20.22-23; Mark 10.38-40; Luke 12.50), Jesus' suffering and death are described as a baptism which his disciples will come to share. This is no metaphorical use of the word 'baptism', but a true indication of the implications of the evangelists' understanding of Jesus' baptism by John. Baptism prepares Christians for their life as disciples of Jesus and to face suffering in his name, just as it prepared Jesus for his ministry as a teacher and for the suffering which he would undergo.

Thus, baptism is an incorporation or an adoption of Christians as sons of God (cf. Paul's statement in Romans 8.15 — the Spirit of adoption which enables Christians to pray, 'Abba, Father'), and Jesus' baptism is a model for Christians' experience of baptism just as his life is a model for Christian life. The question is sometimes asked, why did the early Church preserve the custom of baptism, whereas another important ritual of initiation derived from Judaism — circumcision — was eventually abandoned? A simple answer to this question may be, because Jesus himself was baptized, a theologically significant act, and early Christians understood their baptism in relation to his.

Baptism and Jesus' Death and Resurrection

Another way of thinking about baptism which we find in early Christian theology is based on Paul, and particularly Romans 6.3-11. Here Paul writes, 'Do you not know that all of us who have been baptized into Christ Jesus were baptized into his death?', and goes on to explain that this incorporation into Jesus' death means in turn a sharing in his resurrection, which demands that Christians consider themselves 'dead to sin'.

What lies behind this is that being immersed in water and coming up out of it are a powerful symbol of death, burial in the grave, and resurrection. (This way of thinking about water is an Old Testament theme, found particularly in the Psalms, where waters symbolize all that can overwhelm and oppress the faithful worshipper of God, and are thus something from which God needs to supply deliverance: Psalms 18.16; 32.6; 46.3; 69.1-2, 14; 124.4; 144.7). So in this way of looking at baptism the place of Jesus is that of the Lord who died and rose again, and the salvation conveyed by undergoing the symbolic experience of submersion and emergence from water in baptism is resurrection and eternal life with him.

Baptism and Rebirth

A third way of understanding baptism, though often associated with the second because it draws on a similar idea of water as a symbol of renewal, is baptism as new birth or new life, based on John 3.3-5, where Jesus speaks of being born of 'water and the spirit', which was often taken as a reference to baptism by early Christians. The biblical image of baptism as rebirth (or regeneration) is found in the *Apostolic Tradition* (22), where it occurs in the post-baptismal prayer which was quoted earlier, and in Justin's account of baptism in *First Apology,* 61.

Of these ways of thinking about baptism the first two are both strongly focused on Jesus, but one emphasizes the sharing of the gifts from God which Jesus received — the Holy Spirit, sonship, and preparation for ministry — while the other consists in thinking more of sharing in the effects of Christ's death and resurrection. In most early Christian theologians all three ways are woven together into a more complex theological exploration of the biblical images and symbols connected

151

with baptism: Justin and the *Apostolic Tradition* are rather unusual in that they concentrate on the idea of regeneration alone.

So the point to underline is the way in which these different ways of thinking about baptism are tied in different ways to the figure of Jesus, and particularly the importance of the story of Jesus' baptism in the Gospels for how Christians thought generally about baptism. Since this is not always sufficiently stressed in modern books on the theology of baptism, it is important to bear in mind that when they were being baptized, early Christians were imitating what Jesus had undergone, and were expecting to be identified with their Lord in some way in the life that they were going to live — more strongly perhaps than at any other point in their Christian life.

Jesus and the Eucharist

As we have seen in an earlier section, the early Church's development of the theology and liturgy of the Eucharist was based to a large extent on Jesus' words of institution, identifying the eucharistic bread and wine as his body and blood and telling his disciples to 'Do this' (share bread and wine), 'in remembrance of me' (1 Cor. 11.24-25). However, it should be borne in mind that the context of Jesus' words to his disciples was probably a passover meal. In Luke's account of the Last Supper, Jesus says to his disciples, 'I have eagerly desired to eat this Passover with you before I suffer; for I tell you, I will not eat it until it is fulfilled in the kingdom of God' (Luke 22.15-16, NRSV). The fact that in Luke 22.17-19, Jesus blesses the cup of wine before the bread also confirms that the Last Supper (at least in Luke's interpretation) was a passover meal, since the sharing of a cup of wine before the meal proper was characteristic of the Jewish passover ritual.

Eucharist and Passover

This raises an interesting question. Did the prayers used at the passover meal influence Christian eucharistic prayers? While scholars have given varied answers to this question, there is one early Christian source whose eucharistic prayers clearly seem to echo Jewish prayers of thanksgiving at meals, such as would have been used at the passover.

This is the *Didache,* parts of whose eucharistic prayers are quoted in the box.

The Eucharistic Prayers of the *Didache*

And concerning the eucharist, give thanks in this manner. First concerning the cup: 'We thank you, our Father, for the holy vine of David, your son, which you have made known to us through Jesus, your son. Glory be to you for ever'. And concerning the broken bread: 'We thank you, our Father, for the life and knowledge which you have made known to us through Jesus, your son. Glory be to you for ever. As this bread that is broken was scattered upon the mountains, and gathered together, and became one, so let your church be gathered together from the ends of the earth into your kingdom: for yours is the glory and the power through Jesus Christ for ever.'

(Section 9; *New Eusebius,* p. 10)

And after you are filled, give thanks thus: 'We thank you, Holy Father, for your holy name, which you have made to dwell in our hearts, and for the knowledge, faith, and immortality, which you have made known to us through Jesus, your son. Glory be to you for ever [. . .] Remember, Lord, your church, to deliver her from all evil, and to perfect her in your love, and gather together from the four winds her that is sanctified into your kingdom which you have prepared for her. For yours is the power and the glory for ever'.

(Section 10; *New Eusebius,* p. 10)

The two paragraphs were probably originally distinct but similar eucharistic prayers, which the author of the *Didache* has arranged so that one is used before and one after the bread and wine are eaten. Each prayer consists of a short series of expressions of thanksgiving or petition (which comes last and takes the form of a prayer for the Church), punctuated by a refrain which ascribes glory to God.

It seems very likely that these prayers are modelled on Jewish prayers at meals. Jewish prayers thanked God for creating the world and for granting the land of Israel to his people, and concluded with a petition for blessing (see the quotations from Jewish prayers in Jasper and Cuming, *Prayers of the Eucharist*, pp. 7-12). What we see in the *Didache* is that such prayers have been Christianized to refer to God's gift of salvation through Jesus and to the Church. It is not surprising that as Jewish Christians prayed the meal prayers with which they were familiar, they would have adapted them to refer to what was central to their own faith, the figure of Jesus as Lord and as the bringer of salvation.

Although the prayers of the *Didache* mention Jesus as Son of God and speak of him as the bringer of life and knowledge, they do not refer to his death, nor allude to obedience to Jesus' command at the Last Supper to 'Do this' as the basis for the Christian Eucharist. Nevertheless, commemoration of what Jesus has done for Christians is central to the prayers. Thus, even when the Last Supper is not envisaged as the authority for what is being done, it is still the case that the sharing of a meal of bread and wine is intimately related to Christians' perception of what Jesus had done on their behalf.

Later Developments in Eucharistic Theology

The *Didache* is unique among surviving early Christian texts; the *Apostolic Tradition* is more typical of how eucharistic liturgy and theology were to develop in later centuries. As we have already seen, its eucharistic prayer incorporates several features — an institution narrative, remembrance of Jesus' death and resurrection, and act of offering to God — which are found in almost all later eucharistic prayers. The institution narrative, in particular, helps to serve as a warrant or justification for what is being done in the Eucharist as an act of obedience to Jesus' explicit command (even though, as we can see from the example of the *Didache*, the Eucharist could have continued to develop without this element being made explicit).

It was another step, not completed until the fourth century (though Justin's words about the institution narrative in *First Apology*, 66 are already quite close), to hold that it was the quotation of Jesus' words 'This is my body' and 'This is my blood' which actually effected the consecration or transformation of the bread and wine into his body and blood, and therefore made the Eucharist valid. But once this interpretation of Jesus' words had begun to hold sway, the way was open for another important theological development connected with the idea of the Eucharist as a sacrifice.

Eucharistic Sacrifice

Because the Eucharist was linked by the words of institution to Jesus' death, it could be seen particularly as a commemoration of his death, rather than a more general thanksgiving for his life and the salvation he offered. Meanwhile, the Eucharist was already regarded as a kind of offering or sacrifice because of the significance with which Christians invested the idea of their worship as part of a life of pure or spiritual sacrifice (see above, p. 143).

Once these ideas were combined, the way was open to the idea of the Eucharist as a sacrifice in which Jesus' death on the cross is offered to God by the minister of the Eucharist as a sacrifice for sin. Already by the middle of the third century, interpretations of the Eucharist in these terms were being offered, as by Cyprian:

> If Christ Jesus, our Lord and God, is himself the high priest of God the Father, and first offered himself as a sacrifice to the Father, and commanded this to be done in remembrance of himself, then assuredly the priest acts truly in Christ's stead, when he reproduces what Christ did, and he then offers a true and complete sacrifice to God the Father, if he begins to offer as he sees Christ himself has offered. (*Letter* 63.14; Bettenson, *Early Christian Fathers*, p. 272)

From this point, the doctrine of the Eucharist as a sacrifice gradually grew stronger, to the point where in the Catholic Church of the Middle Ages it was widely accepted that in the Eucharist the sacrifice of Christ on the cross really was being offered again for the particular community or the particular purposes for which the Eucharist was being celebrated.

That was not an early Christian development, but nevertheless interpretations of the place of Jesus in the Eucharist in the early Church were closely connected, at least from the time of Cyprian, to the development of the doctrine of the principal act of Christian worship as an act of sacrifice. Among Protestant Christians, the challenge to the doctrine of eucharistic sacrifice issued by the sixteenth-century Reformation led to a new emphasis on the Eucharist as a remembrance or memorial of Jesus' death, while in more recent times the churches, both Catholic and Protestant, have, as was pointed out at the beginning of this chapter, made an attempt to recover and understand something of the meaning of worship in the early Church.

Jesus — Divine and Human

This chapter looks at the doctrines of the Trinity and the incarnation as they took shape over the first four centuries of the Church in the work of individual theologians such as Justin, Origen, Athanasius, and the Cappadocian Fathers and in the doctrinal statements of the Councils of Nicaea and Chalcedon, which represented the collective (if not the unanimous) theological mind of the Church.

Most theologians of the early Church took the divinity of Jesus for granted on the basis of the New Testament evidence; the questions which some people today might reasonably want to ask, such as whether the historical evidence for Jesus' miraculous birth, fulfilment of prophecy, miracles, and resurrection is reliable enough to serve as proof of his divine status, did not often trouble them. Even so sophisticated a theologian as Origen, who was aware of arguments against Christian belief in Jesus such as those put forward by the pagan scholar Celsus, rested his case for Jesus' divinity on the evidence of his miracles and fulfilment of prophecy.

However, theologians of the early Church needed to show that belief in Jesus' divinity was reasonable, rather than irrational or foolish (Origen was particularly concerned to do this), and to explore its theological implications. For example, they had to decide whether Jesus was a divine being distinct from the Father (which posed the potentially disturbing question of whether there were in fact two Gods), or only an appearance or power of the Father (which would preserve belief in one God more easily); and they had to decide on the implications of Jesus' divinity for the interpretation of his nature as a human being: was Jesus only apparently human, partly human, or wholly human as well as divine?

Not all early Christians answered these questions in ways which were orthodox (that is, 'right-thinking') in terms of the decisions made by the fourth- and fifth-century councils; some held views which were condemned either at the time or retrospectively as heresy (that is, as an individual 'choice' or 'opinion' rather than the faith of the Church).

The history of theology is littered with formidable-sounding technical terms such as 'docetism', 'adoptionism', 'monarchianism', 'patripassionism', and 'Sabellianism' — not to mention the fourth- and fifth-century heresies of Arianism, Apollinarianism, and Nestorianism — which help scholars to categorize the different interpretations of the divinity and humanity of Jesus which were current in the early Church. The terminology is testimony to a lively debate among Christians which began as early as the second century, many of whose details are still of interest today.

The Beginnings of Debate

The Humanity of Jesus

Near the beginning of the second century, Ignatius of Antioch wrote of Jesus as 'God in man, true life in death, son of Mary and son of God' (*Ephesians,* 7; *New Eusebius,* p. 13). His explicit references to Jesus as God go further than anything found in the New Testament. But he was confident of Jesus' humanity as well as his divinity — that his human birth and suffering on the cross were compatible with speaking of him as of divine origin, God's Son before he became human: he even described Jesus' death as 'the passion of my God' (*Romans,* 6).

Ignatius, however, knew Christians who denied that Jesus was born, ate and drank like an ordinary human being, or really suffered and died on the cross (*Trallians,* 9-10; *New Eusebius,* pp. 14-15). The existence of such views — known as docetism — shows that some second-century Christians found it hard to reconcile belief in Jesus' humanity and divinity, and gave his divinity priority. Docetism is also condemned by the first letter of John (4.2-3) which, though part of the New Testament, may be of similar date to Ignatius' letters.

Docetist views evidently persisted for some time in the Church, since they are criticized by a number of second-century theologians after Ignatius. They were also typical of some of the gnostic versions of Christianity which were important rivals to what gradually became established as orthodox Christian teaching.

> **Gnostic/gnosticism**: terms applied to a range of beliefs current in the second century. Gnosticism typically rejected the idea that the world was created by the supreme God and often treated it as the work of an inferior or ignorant creator. Jesus is a messenger from the supreme God who enters this world to offer human beings knowledge (Greek, *gnosis*) of the heavenly realm, by means of which they are freed from the creator's control.

The second-century gnostic leader Basilides is alleged to have believed that Jesus was an 'incorporeal power' who could change his appearance at will, and that it was Simon of Cyrene, not Jesus, who was crucified (cf. the account from Irenaeus, *Against Heresies*, 1.19, in *New Eusebius*, pp. 76-78). By the majority of theologians, however, docetic views were rejected as clearly contrary to the Gospel portrayal of Jesus' human life and suffering.

Jesus as God's Word

As we saw in Chapter 1, one of the most important ways in which second-century theologians understood Jesus was as God's Word — in Greek, *logos*, which may also be translated 'speech' or 'reason'. The title Logos is found in John's Gospel and is used by Ignatius, for whom Jesus is '[God's] son, who is his Word, coming forth from silence, who in all things did the good pleasure of him that sent him' (*Magnesians*, 8; *New Eusebius*, p. 14). But the idea that Jesus was God's Word really became established only in the work of Justin and other Christian apologists of the mid- to late-second century.

To identify Jesus with God's Logos, which had been understood by

---

Justin on the Logos
(Bettenson, *Early Christian Fathers*, pp. 60, 62-63)

Jesus Christ alone has been begotten as the unique Son of God, being already his Word, his First-begotten, and his Power. By the will of God he became man, and gave us this teaching for the conversion and restoration of mankind.

(First Apology, 23)

[God's] Son (who alone is properly called Son, the Word who is with God and is begotten before the creation, when in the beginning God created and ordered all things through him), is called Christ.

(Second Apology, 5)

Whatever has been spoken aright by anyone belongs to us Christians; for we worship and love, next to God, the Logos which is from the unbegotten and ineffable God; since it was on our behalf that he has been made man, that, becoming par-taker of our sufferings, he may also bring us healing. For all those [pagan] writers were able, through the seed of the Logos implanted in them, to see reality darkly.

(Second Apology, 13)

Middle Platonist philosophers as a divine power or ordering principle active throughout creation, was the boldest theological move of sec-ond-century Christianity. Its consequence was that Jesus was held to be at the centre of all of God's activity in creation and his relations with human beings. The same divine Word through which God created the universe, and which he used to communicate to human beings through the prophets and by means of his revelations to Abraham and Moses in the Old Testament — that same Word is also the one who became incarnate and spoke to human beings in Jesus, sharing our sufferings, teaching, and healing, as Justin says.

The doctrine of the Logos thus helped Christians to position Jesus intellectually as well as experientially at the centre of their faith. As well as being the risen Lord who guided and governed the Church, they could see Jesus as the focus of all God's dealings with human beings, his life as the moment in history in which God's communication came in its clearest form. As Irenaeus put it, God's 'true nature and immensity cannot be discovered or described by his creatures. But he is by no means unknown to them. For through his Word all his creatures learn that there is one God, the Father, who controls all things, and gives existence to all' (*Against Heresies*, 4.20; Bettenson, *Early Christian Fathers*, p. 75).

The Logos-doctrine also possessed an apologetic value. It helped to show that Christian teachings about Jesus were in continuity with the revelation of God in the Old Testament — which was a useful argument in debate with Jews (Justin's *Dialogue with Trypho* centres largely on this point) and gnostics, many of whom rejected the Old Testament as the revelation of an inferior God, the creator of the material world, not the supreme God who was the Father of Jesus. Justin also found the Logos-doctrine very useful in his polemic against paganism. By seeing the Logos as active before the incarnation, not only in the biblical story of God's revelation, but elsewhere in human religion and culture, wherever human beings sought the truth about God, Justin could claim (see box on page 160) that everything of value which was taught by pagan philosophers belonged to Christianity — was part of the revelation of God completed in Jesus. The errors of the pagans, of course, were their own misinterpretations or distortions of the truth which they had received.

The Word a Second God?

The Logos is a mediator between God the Father (who is himself invisible and beyond human understanding) and creation, God's agent or assistant, through whom he created the world. Does this mean that the Logos is a second God besides the Father?

Justin and several other early theologians did not shrink from speaking about the Word in this way, as 'another God' or 'a second God'. Provided that the priority of the Father as the source of all divine being and power was preserved, they did not think that the monothe-

---

The Logos as Mediator

The Word was made the minister of the Father's grace to man, for man's benefit. For man he wrought his redemptive work, displaying God to man, and man to God. He safeguarded the invisibility of the Father, lest man should ever become contemptuous of God, and that man should always have some goal to which he might advance. At the same time he displayed God in visible form to men through his many acts of mediation, lest man should be utterly remote from God and so cease to be.

(Irenaeus, *Against Heresies*, 4.20; Bettenson, *Early Christian Fathers*, pp. 75-76)

---

ism to which Christians were committed was threatened. But other writers, such as Irenaeus, preferred not to use this language, and placed more emphasis on the unity of Father and Son. The term 'Logos' implied that the Son was an aspect of the Father's own mind or being which could be distinguished from him (as human speech is distinguished from the thought which gives rise to it) but never separated from him. As yet, therefore, Christian theologians did not always think of Father and Son as clearly distinct divine persons; the general acceptance of this idea was a development of the third century.

Alternatives to Logos-Theology

Although talking of Jesus as another or a second God besides the Father was eventually to be dropped from the vocabulary of Christian orthodoxy, the doctrine of Jesus as the Logos formed the basis of the doctrine of the Trinity as it developed in the third and fourth centuries. In the second century, however, there were still alternative views of Jesus on offer.

Adoptionism — Jesus as Merely Human

Justin knew Christians who believed that Jesus was not the pre-existent Son of God but a human being who was chosen by God to be Messiah or Christ (*Dialogue with Trypho,* 48). Such views persisted later in the second century, when they are particularly associated with two leaders called Theodotus, both of whom were active in Rome. The Theodotians denied Jesus' divinity, and maintained that he was a righteous man (i.e., he obeyed the Jewish Law) on whom God's spirit or power descended at his baptism. They further claimed that this had been the traditional teaching of the Roman church until late in the second century, and that it was only after that time that Jesus began to be called God (cf. *New Eusebius,* pp. 143-5).

Views like this are usually referred to as 'adoptionism', on the grounds that they deny that Jesus was Son of God from birth. Second-century adoptionists were probably motivated by a desire to take seriously the Gospel witness to Jesus' obedience to the Father, and his baptism as effecting a change in his status before God. It should be noted, however, that not all adoptionists denied that Jesus was born of a virgin — they could consistently maintain that his birth was miraculous and marked him out as a special human being, though not divine. Nor is it the case that all adoptionists were Jewish Christians who obeyed the Old Testament Law and were committed to viewing the Messiah as a human being — though some (known from the second century as Ebionites) probably did have this background. It was open to anyone who disliked the doctrine of the Logos as implying the existence of a second God to take up adoptionist views.

Monarchianism — Jesus as the Father in Person

Another group of theologians who did not take readily to the doctrine of the Logos are known as the monarchians. A monarchian leader called Noetus taught in Smyrna in Asia Minor at the end of the second century. Like adoptionism, monarchianism also seems to have been the view held by some members of the church in Rome, where it became known as 'Sabellianism' after Sabellius, an early third-century theologian about whom, however, very little is known.

The basis of Noetus' doctrine seems to have been that Jesus was

> **Monarchianism** (or **Sabellianism**): belief in the unity of God, involving rejection of the idea that the Logos or Son of God is a distinct divine being rather than a power or aspect of the Father. 'Monarchianism' is from Greek, *monos* 'only' and *arche* 'rule' — implying that God does not share his rule over creation with another divine being.

the Father himself, made visible, not a separate divine person. Probably he did not think it was possible to explain the incarnation rationally in terms drawn from philosophy (which is one of the things that the Logos-doctrine attempted to do); he was simply unhappy with the implication of the Logos-doctrine that there could be a divinity distinct from that of the Father. Noetus' opponents, however, were quick to seize on one apparent consequence of his teaching, and to accuse him of what became known as the heresy of 'patripassianism' (cf. *New Eusebius*, pp. 145-46).

> **Patripassianism**: the doctrine that the Father himself underwent suffering (Latin, *passio*) on the cross — a corollary of the view that the divinity of Jesus is the visible appearance of the Father's divinity, and not distinct from it.

The Contribution of Tertullian

At the beginning of the third century Tertullian wrote *Against Praxeas,* a defence of the doctrine of the Logos and refutation of monarchian and patripassianist views. In order to defend the Logos-doctrine, he had to show that the unity of God is not threatened by belief in the Son and the Holy Spirit as distinct divine beings. (Tertullian is one of the first theologians to expand discussion of the relationship between Father and Son to take the Holy Spirit into account, and thus to make his theology explicitly Trinitarian.)

To do this, Tertullian devised some theological terminology

which has endured to the present day: he referred to the Trinity as three persons who share the same divine substance. Three divine persons, he argued, can share one divine nature or substance equally, without dividing it, but nevertheless in such a way that they are truly distinct from one another. The unity of the substance answers the monarchians' fear that the Logos-theology threatens monotheism; the distinction of persons ensures that the pitfalls of patripassianism are avoided. To make certain of refuting patripassianism, Tertullian also argued that in Jesus there are two natures, divine and human, and that it is only the human nature which suffers, not the divine Word (*Against Praxeas*, 29; Bettenson, *Early Christian Fathers*, pp. 122-23). This distinction was to become an important source of disagreement in the fifth century.

The following passage is characteristic of how Tertullian tries to capture the complex relationship, involving both identity and difference, between Father and Son:

> All are of one [Godhead], that is, through unity of substance; while this still safeguards the mystery of the 'economy', which disposes the unity into a Trinity, arranging in order the three persons, Father, Son, and Holy Spirit, though these are three not in quality but in degree, not in substance but in form, not in power but in manifestation [. . .] because God is one and from him those degrees and forms are assigned. (*Against Praxeas*, 2; Bettenson, *Early Christian Fathers*, p. 134)

Economy: a Greek word borrowed into Latin by Tertullian, meaning the 'arrangement' by which (in his view) the divine monarchy or rule over creation is shared among the three persons without being divided.

With Tertullian's work (his defence of the doctrine of the Logos and his inclusion of the Holy Spirit in the same theological scheme), the first phase of debate over the doctrine of the Trinity may be said to have come to an end. The doctrine of Jesus as the divine Logos become human was well established, and docetic, adoptionist, and patripassianist views had been largely rejected by the Church.

Origen and His Successors

Origen's contribution to the doctrine of the Trinity is important but very complex. In many ways his theology is close to Justin's, including the use of the term 'second God' to assert the Son's distinctness from the Father (*Against Celsus*, 5.39). The Logos is God's agent in creation and revelation — and not only this, he is the source of all reason and virtue possessed by created beings, an idea which parallels Justin's belief that all truth, wherever human beings discover it, is the result of the activity of the Logos. But in these and other areas, Origen develops the doctrine of the Logos in a new way.

Distinction of Persons

Origen was aware of the monarchian ideas of the previous century and keen to refute them. The distinction between Father and Son is not one of appearance only, it is a distinction of 'existence' or 'reality' — in Greek, *hypostasis*, a very difficult term to translate.

> *Hypostasis*: one of the most important technical terms in patristic theology, especially from the fourth century. In contexts where it refers to the distinction between Father and Son it is often convenient to translate it 'person', but it is really a much more abstract term than this, one that simply does the job of asserting that something truly exists.

If the Father and Son are truly existing beings, how are they related to one another, and how does the Son reveal the Father? Origen writes:

> They are two distinct *hypostases*, but one in mental unity, in agreement, and in identity of will. Thus he who has seen the Son, who is 'an effulgence of the glory and express image of the *hypostasis*' of God [Heb. 1.3], has seen God in him who is God's image. (*Against Celsus*, 8.12; Chadwick, *Origen Contra Celsum*, pp. 460-61)

There are two ideas in this passage which are characteristic of Origen's thinking on the Trinity. The first is that the unity of Father and Son is a unity of mind and will; Origen does not think that John 10.30 ('I and the Father are one') requires theologians to assert anything more than this — indeed to do so is dangerous, since it risks denying the distinction of *hypostasis* and playing into the hands of the monarchians.

The second idea is that the Son is the image of the Father. Origen found this biblical term (cf. Col. 1.15) the most useful way of asserting both similarity and difference between Father and Son. The concept of image allows the Son to share in the Father's attributes (such as goodness and wisdom), while at the same being distinct from him; it also shows the priority of the Father, even when he brings into being a Son who is in many ways equal to himself:

> The God and Father of the universe is not the only being who is great; for he gave a share of himself and his greatness to the only-begotten and firstborn of all creation, that being himself an image of the invisible God he might preserve the image of the Father also in respect of his greatness. For it was impossible that, so to speak, a rightly proportioned and beautiful image of the invisible God should not also show the image of his greatness. (*Against Celsus*, 6.69; Chadwick, *Origen Contra Celsum*, p. 383)

Subordinationism

In the fourth century, when the Council of Nicaea had defined the unity of Father and Son as one of substance (Greek, *ousia*), Origen's doctrine of the Son as image of God came to be seen by many theologians as an inadequate account of the Son's equality to the Father, and his doctrine of the Trinity was condemned as subordinationist — that is, as teaching that the Son and the Holy Spirit are inferior to the Father.

It is true that Origen maintains the existence of a hierarchy of divine beings, with the Father as the originator of the Son and Spirit and superior to them in certain respects, rather than a strictly equal Trinity (cf. Bettenson, *Early Christian Fathers*, pp. 232-35 for examples from Origen's writings). However, Origen did not intend to denigrate the Son or deny his divinity (or that of the Spirit): the doctrine of the image does not mean that the Son is a crude copy of the Father, but a reflection who mirrors his qualities. The Son, Origen says, even mirrors the 'invisibility' of the Father (*Against Celsus*, 6.69) — i.e., the fact that the Father is difficult for the human mind to perceive. When he wished to reveal himself, God did not send an inferior being whose nature it would be easy for humans to grasp, but his own Son, through whom he had made the world. Even in the person of Jesus, to understand the revelation of God requires self-discipline and intellectual effort. (Origen, it will be remembered from Chapter 6, was highly ascetic in his attitude to Christian life.)

Eternal Generation

Origen believed that the Father brought the Son into being before the beginning of time — there was never a moment when the Father was without his Son. Not all early theologians believed this; Tertullian, for example, seems to have thought that the Logos became a person distinct from the Father only when God chose to create the world with his aid (*Against Praxeas*, 5-7; Bettenson, *Early Christian Fathers*, pp. 118-20), and Justin probably held a similar view. Origen rejected any such idea because it was suggestive of change in God, which conflicted with belief in divine impassibility, a doctrine which he had adopted under the influence of Platonist philosophy.

> **Impassibility of God**: the doctrine that God is incapable of change or suffering of any sort, including experiencing any change or limit to his being or nature, or any sharing of human experiences of physical or mental pain, limitations on knowledge, or fear of mortality.

Even the belief that the Son existed eternally with the Father, however, was not sufficient for Origen. He argued that the bringing into being (in traditional language, generation or begetting) of the Son by the Father did not take place at one moment — even an inconceivably long time ago, before time as we know it began — but is to be conceived of as an eternal relationship, something which is always in process but never completed. Origen acknowledged that speaking in this way was difficult to comprehend, since in talking of human beings or animals, we do not understand the relationship of Father to Son in this way. As Origen wrote in his *On First Principles,* his most important work:

> Human thought cannot comprehend how the unbegotten God be-comes the Father of the only-begotten Son. For it is an eternal and ceaseless generation, as radiance is generated from light. (*On First Principles,* 1.2; Bettenson, *Early Christian Fathers,* p. 231)

Origen believed (wrongly as it happens) that the sun produces light eternally at no loss to itself (he did not know that the sun has only a finite supply of hydrogen as fuel); this made the relationship of a source of light such as the sun to the radiance which it gives off a suit-able analogy for the notion of a God who is always bringing into being a Son without any loss to himself, any diminution of his power, any change in his nature.

This doctrine of eternal generation, as it is called, was to become an established part of orthodox theology in the fourth century. While supporting the notion of the unchangeability of God, it also made the Father's relationship with his Son a feature of his nature: having a Son is part of what it means for God to be who he is, not something he could have chosen to do or not to do. Views such as that of Tertullian are abandoned.

The Third Century after Origen

In the years after Origen's death in 254 there were two instances of con-troversy over the doctrine of the Logos. One of these was a revival of a form of adoptionism by Paul of Samosata, a Bishop of Antioch who was condemned for his teaching by two councils of bishops, the later in 268. The exact character of Paul's views is not entirely clear, but he seems to have held that Jesus was a human being who was indwelt or inspired by the divine Logos, perhaps believing that the Logos was not a distinct person but only a power of God.

The second controversy is more significant, in that it concerns a theologian who was a follower of Origen, but who did not succeed in maintaining Origen's balance between the distinctness of the Son from the Father and the similarity or likeness between the two. Dionysius of Alexandria (bishop 247-64) was accused by his namesake Dionysius of Rome (bishop 259-68) of failing to believe that the Father, Son, and Holy Spirit were one *hypostasis,* and of using language which implied that the Son of God was a created being (effectively, an angel) rather than divine (see *New Eusebius,* pp. 252-53). Dionysius of Alexandria denied these charges, but it is likely that in his teaching about the Logos, he had moved away from Origen's doctrine of the eternal generation of the Son as God's image to a more subordinationist position. On the other hand, Dionysius of Rome's views show that not all theologians were happy with Origen's belief in the distinct *hypostases* of Father, Son, and Holy Spirit, or Tertullian's language of three persons. These disagreements set the scene for the Trinitarian controversy of the fourth century.

The Council of Nicaea and the Fourth Century

The Theology of Arius

The controversy which led to the Council of Nicaea was prompted by the Alexandrian theologian Arius, a priest whose views came into conflict with those of his bishop, Alexander (Bishop of Alexandria 312-28). The label 'Arian controversy' is convenient for the dispute, though it continued long after Arius' death (in 336). Arius' views are known only from a few short letters and an extract from a theological poem (the *Thalia*) which he wrote during the controversy, but these are sufficient to show the nature of his teaching (see *New Eusebius,* pp. 324-27, 330-31, on which the following is based).

Arius rejected the belief that the Son of God is 'co-eternal' with the Father and argued that he must have come into being at some point, before which he did not exist. The Father generated the Son by an act of will and (like the universe) 'out of nothing'. It was logical for Arius to go on to maintain that the Son was a created being. Arius emphasized this because he did not believe that the Son shared the Father's own nature: to accept this would be to divide God, and to maintain that there were 'two unoriginated beings' — i.e., two supreme

Gods, which is impossible to reconcile with monotheism. He also denied that the Son is 'of one substance' or 'consubstantial' (Greek *homoousios*) with the Father.

It is clear that Arius' motive was to maintain the unity of God and the uniqueness of the Father. This does not mean that he refused to call the Son 'God' or maintained that he is a creature 'like us', for example in being 'changeable' or capable of sin (though Arius' opponents were quick to make this charge). The Son is superior to human beings in every way, a 'perfect creature'. He is a mediator between God and creation, through whom human beings receive the blessings of salvation, but he does not share in God's nature or qualities, and he himself knows the Father only imperfectly, not as the Father knows himself.

Arius on the Son as Mediator

God then himself is in essence ineffable to all.
He alone has neither equal nor like, none comparable in glory.
We call him Unbegotten because of the one in
    nature begotten;
We raise hymns to him as unbegun because of him
    who has beginning;
We adore him as eternal because of the one born in time.
The Unbegun appointed the Son to be Beginning of things
    begotten [. . .]
He has nothing proper to God in his essential property,
for neither is he equal nor yet consubstantial with him.

(The *Thalia; New Eusebius,* pp. 330-31)

The Council of Nicaea

From being a local dispute between a priest who accused his bishop of the 'heresy' of maintaining the eternal generation of the Son, the Arian controversy became an issue of concern to the whole Church because Arius appealed for support outside Egypt, to bishops in Palestine and Asia Minor.

Shortly after this (in 324), the Emperor Constantine, who had shared control of the Roman empire since 306, became sole ruler, in charge of the Eastern provinces for the first time. Constantine had been converted to Christianity in 312 and since then had already intervened in disputes between different parties of Christians in the Western provinces of the empire (particularly in North Africa). His goal in the East was to ensure that the Church remained united, and that the emperor was not faced with the problem of deciding between competing groups of Christians all claiming imperial favour.

It was Constantine himself who summoned over 200 bishops to attend the Council of Nicaea in Bythinia in Asia Minor in May 325. Because of its size and because it was the first Church council to set out a creed to be assented to by all bishops, the Council of Nicaea was eventually to be accepted as the first general or ecumenical council of the Church, its authority in theory binding on all Christians.

The Creed

Although three accounts of the Council of Nicaea written by participants have survived, along with a number of letters and a list of 'canons' or rulings made by the bishops (see *New Eusebius*, pp. 338-44), they do not give a complete picture, so it is far from clear what debates actually took place. The best evidence we have for the doctrinal position of the council is the creed itself, which all of the bishops present were asked to sign.

Though it is based on the sort of creed used in baptismal liturgies (see Chapter 7), the creed of Nicaea is modified to take account of Arius' teachings, which are listed explicitly in the 'anathemas' (condemned propositions) attached to the end. (These anathemas replaced most of the third article of the creed, concerning the Holy Spirit and the Church, which were not the focus of debate at Nicaea.) Several points in the creed underline the rejection of Arius' views: the Son is 'from the substance of the Father' — i.e., he is not 'from nothing' but shares in God's own nature and being; and he is 'begotten, not made' — i.e., he is different from all creatures; to call him God's Son is not a figure of speech, but an indication of a unique relationship to the Father which does not depend on the Father's will in the same way as the relationship of creatures to God.

The Creed of Nicaea (325)

We believe in one God, the Father almighty,
maker of all things, both seen and unseen;

and in one Lord Jesus Christ,
the Son of God,
begotten of the Father,
only-begotten;
that is, from the substance of the Father,
God from God, light from light, true God from true God,
begotten, not made,
of one substance *(homoousios)* with the Father;
through whom all things came to be,
both in heaven and on earth;
who for us men and for our salvation came down
and was made flesh, became man,
suffered, and rose on the third day,
and ascended to heaven,
and is coming to judge the living and the dead;

and in the Holy Spirit.

But as for those who say, 'There was when he was not'
and, 'Before he was begotten he was not',
and pretend that the Son of God came to be out of nothing,
or is from another *hypostasis* or substance *(ousia)*,
or is changeable or alterable,
these the catholic and apostolic Church anathematizes.

The Significance of 'Homoousios'

The most important word in the creed, however, is *homoousios*, 'of one substance', probably the most famous word in the history of Christian doctrine. It implies the unity of nature or being of Father and Son — the idea developed by Tertullian to assert that the unity of God does not conflict with the existence of three divine persons. As we have seen, this notion was not employed by Origen, who preferred to speak of the unity of Father and Son as a unity of mind or will; it was rejected explicitly by Arius, and also by Dionysius of Alexandria (whose namesake Dionysius of Rome attacks him for this). By employing a term previously rejected by these three Alexandrian theologians, the Council of Nicaea changed the course of Christian doctrine, ensuring that the unity and equality of Father and Son would take precedence over any form of subordinationism, or the wish (in Arius' case) to safeguard the uniqueness of the Father and downgrade the Son to the status of a creature.

After Nicaea

The creed of Nicaea was accepted by all but a few of the bishops present — two of the objectors were bishops from Libya (in the jurisdiction of the Bishop of Alexandria) who were probably personal friends of Arius. In the light of this success, it is at first sight surprising that the council did not end the Arian controversy, but provoked severe criticism which led to nearly half a century of disagreement.

Not all of this disagreement was doctrinally motivated — personal rivalry and local loyalties often played a part. Once disputes between groups of bishops had begun to develop, they often assumed a momentum of their own, so that the history of the Church in the period from Nicaea to the second of the ecumenical councils, at the imperial capital of Constantinople in 381, can often give the impression of being a series of squabbles between competing 'church parties', striving for power in the Church.

Problems over Terminology

Where doctrinal problems did exist, however, they can be described in terms of attitudes to the key terms *homoousios* and *hypostasis*. The word *homoousios* remained unpopular with many theologians for the same reason as Arius had disliked it: it suggested that the distinction between Father and Son was a result of a division in the being of God, or, if this was denied, made it difficult to believe in any real distinction between Father and Son at all. It did not help that one keen supporter of Nicaea and the *homoousios,* Bishop Marcellus of Ancyra, was accused with some plausibility of reviving the heresies of Sabellius and Paul of Samosata (see above, pp. 163-64, 169).

The problem over the word *hypostasis* was that most bishops in the East had been used to using this term as Origen had, to describe the distinction of the three persons of the Trinity. In the anathemas attached to the creed of Nicaea, however, the term is used as a synonym for 'substance' *(ousia),* with the implication that 'of one substance' *(homoousios)* means that the Trinity is to be understood as one *hypostasis* — one individual thing, or even one person.

A church council which met at Antioch in 341 illustrates the attitude of many Eastern bishops. The creeds of this council (cf. *Creeds, Councils and Controversies,* pp. 8-11) condemn Arius' teaching in terms similar to the anathemas of Nicaea, but ignore the word *homoousios* and guardedly assert the distinction of *hypostasis* between Father, Son, and Holy Spirit.

Following Constantine's death in 337 his son, Constantius II (d. 361) and a later emperor, Valens (364-78) made several attempts to bring the bishops of the empire together to reach agreement on a new creed which would replace Nicaea and avoid the contentious term *ousia.* In the end these attempts failed because sufficient bishops were committed to the terminology of *homoousios* to maintain a successful resistance to the threat of imperial coercion, particularly in the West. General agreement had to await new theological initiatives, not just a compromise between church parties.

Towards Agreement

Theological agreement was mainly the work of Bishop Athanasius of Alexandria and the Cappadocian Fathers (for information about these see Chapter 6).

Athanasius

Athanasius had attended the Council of Nicaea as one of Bishop Alexander's deacons or assistants. Throughout his own career as Bishop of

Alexandria (from 328) he remained an implacable enemy of Arianism and of any theology which failed to support the ideas of Nicaea. In his writings he documents the many attempts of his enemies to produce new creeds which would supplant Nicaea, all of which he rejected. His five periods of exile from Alexandria between 336 and 366 illustrate the hostility of Constantius and Valens to a prominent bishop who refused to toe the line of a compromise solution to the controversy.

While he was committed to the *homoousios,* Athanasius was probably not particularly concerned with giving it a precise meaning by drawing on philosophical definitions of the word 'substance', as did some of his contemporaries. *Homoousios* simply establishes the identity of Father and Son (and Holy Spirit) as regards their degree of divinity and their divine power, so that the Son is not seen as a semi-divine being, inferior to the Father. Athanasius himself was reluctant to talk about a distinction of *hypostasis* between Father, Son, and Spirit, but he was prepared to acknowledge the orthodoxy of those who did so, provided they accepted the *homoousios* and did not hold Arian views (see the letter of a council of Alexandria held in 362, *Creeds, Councils and Controversies,* pp. 80-83). This was a very important step towards reuniting the Church around the creed of Nicaea.

The Cappadocian Fathers

The contribution of the Cappadocian Fathers was in some ways just as important, particularly after Athanasius' death in 373. They not only accepted that talk of three *hypostases* was orthodox, but gave the term a crucial role in affirming an adequate balance between unity and distinction between Father and Son — whereas Nicaea had concentrated rather one-sidedly on unity.

From the time of the Cappadocian Fathers, it is reasonable to translate the Greek word *hypostasis* as 'person', and to speak of the orthodox doctrine of the Trinity as 'three persons in one substance'. (Like Athanasius, the Cappadocians taught the divinity of the Spirit; cf. *Creeds, Councils and Controversies,* pp. 83-85.) This was, of course, in some ways merely a return to the teaching of Origen, though with the term *homoousios* to give added precision to his use of the concept of 'image', and it marked the catching up of Greek theological terminology with the Latin terms already used by Tertullian in the early third century.

The Council of Constantinople (381)

It was the second general or ecumenical council of Constantinople in 381 (summoned by the emperor Theodosius I, a keen supporter of Nicaea) which brought a formal end to the Arian controversy and marked a return to the situation at Nicaea, where all orthodox bishops in theory accepted the same creed. The creed produced by the council was intended to interpret the creed of Nicaea, not to supersede it, but because of its longer second article on the incarnation and fuller statement of the doctrines of the Holy Spirit and the Church it generally came to be preferred.

This is the creed in use in the liturgy of the Eucharist of the Orthodox, Catholic, Anglican, and many other churches today; it is usually known (carelessly) as the 'Nicene' creed or (more accurately) as the 'Nicene-Constantinopolitan' creed. Because of its importance, it is worth reproducing in full, to allow comparison with the original creed of Nicaea (see the box on p. 173). It should be noted that, despite the debates over the word *hypostasis* in the years since 325, the word is not included in the creed; nor is the word *homoousios* applied to the Holy Spirit. An attempt, in other words, is made to avoid controversial terms, even while affirming the achievements of Nicaea, Athanasius, and the Cappadocian Fathers.

The Doctrine of the Person of Christ

The last few pages of this chapter have strayed a long way from the figure of Jesus. This was inevitable, given that belief in his divinity led theologians from the second to the fourth century increasingly to speak of God as Trinity, and to enquire into the implications of this for God's own nature. However, the human side of Jesus was never completely forgotten, and theologians did make an attempt to explain how Jesus could be both divine — the second person of the Trinity come to earth — and human. This is the question usually referred to in theology as the question of 'the person of Christ'.

The Creed of Constantinople (381)

(Differences from the creed of 325 —
mainly additions — are in italics.)

We believe in one God, the Father almighty,
maker *of heaven and earth,*
of all things, both seen and unseen;

and in one Lord Jesus Christ,
the only-begotten Son of God,
who was begotten of the Father before the ages,
light from light, true God from true God,
begotten, not made,
of one substance with the Father;
through whom all things came to be;
who for us men and for our salvation came down *from heaven*
and was made flesh *of the Holy Spirit and the Virgin Mary,*
and became man,

From Origen to Apollinaris

Here again we have to go back to Origen. He gives a very clear account of how he understood the relationship of the divine Logos and the humanity of Jesus in *Against Celsus:*

> We say that this Logos dwelt in the soul of Jesus and was united with it in a closer union than that of any other soul, because [Jesus] alone has been able perfectly to receive the highest participation in him who is the very Logos [= reason] and the very wisdom and the very righteousness itself. (5.39; Chadwick, *Origen Contra Celsum,* p. 296)

The implication of this would seem to be that the human Jesus grew into a closer union with the Logos as he grew closer to God in reason, wisdom, and goodness. Potentially, this could lead to an adoption-

was crucified for us under Pontius Pilate,
and suffered, *and was buried,* and rose on the third day
according to the Scriptures,
and ascended to heaven,
and sits at the right hand of the Father,
and is coming *again with glory* to judge the living
    and the dead;
his kingdom shall have no end;

and in the Holy Spirit,
the Lord and giver of life,
who proceeds from the Father,
who is worshipped and glorified with the Father and the Son,
who spoke through the prophets;

and in one holy Catholic and Apostolic Church.
We confess one baptism for the forgiveness of sins,
we look forward to the resurrection of the dead,
and the life of the coming age. Amen.

ist view of Jesus — he did not become fully Son of God until he had attained a certain moral and spiritual stature. Origen, however, did not mean to imply this. He chooses this way of describing the incarnation only to show that the humanity of Jesus is real: the Logos does not take on the appearance of humanity but is united to a real human being, body and soul, who has a human will and mind with which he does good and serves God.

Because of his union with the Logos, the human Jesus commits no sin but lives a perfect life based on love of virtue. It is as if, Origen says, the soul of Jesus is a piece of iron and the Logos is the fire of a furnace. As iron is heated in a furnace, it takes on the qualities of fire (heat and luminescence); similarly the human soul of Jesus is suffused with divine power and takes on the wisdom and virtue of the Logos to whom he is united, without, however, ceasing to be really human (*On First Principles,* 2.6; Bettenson, *Early Christian Fathers,* pp. 216-17).

Did Jesus Have a Human Soul?

Though Origen had clearly answered this question, not all theologians in the period from his death in 254 to the Council of Constantinople in 381 agreed with him. Strange though it may seem, some preferred the view that the divine Logos dwelt in a human body, effectively taking the place of a human soul in the figure of Jesus.

The reasons for this trend in theology are complex, but one factor is the teaching of Paul of Samosata. Paul had emphasized that the human Jesus was distinct from the Logos who indwelt him, and this was associated with the belief that the Logos was not really a person, but only a power of the Father. An early critic of Paul who debated with him (a theologian called Malchion) answered Paul by comparing the union of Logos and flesh in Jesus to the union of soul and body in a human being (*New Eusebius,* pp. 261-62); perhaps this seemed the best way both of maintaining that the Logos is a person and of combating the implication of Paul's teaching that Jesus was a 'mere human', who just happened (so to speak) to be inspired by God. Jesus, in Malchion's view, was radically different from us.

Fourth-century theologians who followed Malchion's view did not intend to deny that Jesus was human, but they tend to speak of Jesus' humanity as 'flesh' rather than talking about his possession of a human soul (this is true of Athanasius). Clearly there were some fears attached, for the reason I have suggested, to seeing Jesus as a human being with a soul — and therefore thoughts and actions — distinct from those of the divine Logos. Origen's solution to this problem with the metaphor of iron and fire was not much referred to.

The theologian who took this trend to extremes was a supporter of Athanasius' anti-Arian theology, Apollinaris of Laodicea, after whom the heresy of Apollinarianism is named. Whereas Athanasius and some of his contemporaries merely (usually) avoided talk of a human soul in Jesus, Apollinaris explicitly denied that a human soul existed.

Apollinarianism: the view that Jesus did not possess a human soul and therefore was not, in fact, fully human, but the Word dwelling in human flesh.

Apollinaris' view was condemned (in the first canon or ruling of the Council of Constantinople of 381), and all theologians came to accept that Jesus must have possessed a human soul. Gregory of Nazianzus, one of the Cappadocian Fathers, was one of the most important theologians engaged in justifying the rejection of Apollinarianism. His arguments are often summed up in the phrase 'what is not assumed is not healed' (*Creeds, Councils and Controversies*, pp. 88-92): in other words, unless Jesus was a human being like other human beings in every respect (except that he did not commit sin), it cannot be said that human beings have been truly redeemed or offered salvation by his life.

Nestorius and Cyril

Although the question about Jesus' human soul was solved by 381, the problem of the *relationship* between his human and divine natures was not, and further controversies over the person of Christ took place in the fifth century.

Nestorius

Nestorius became Bishop of Constantinople in 428. Like several critics of Apollinaris over the previous half century, he believed that in order to ensure that the divine nature which became man in Jesus was not changed by becoming incarnate, it was necessary to maintain that all of the negative features of Jesus' human life, such as hunger and thirst, fear, ignorance, suffering, and death (everything, in other words, which in the Gospels makes Jesus clearly human, and not just a divine apparition — the docetic view), belonged only to the human Jesus, and were not experienced by the divine Word. To allow that Jesus experienced suffering in his divine nature would open the way either to Arianism — the view that the Word was a creature and not a divine being at all — or to denial of the doctrine of divine impassibility.

Belief in God's impassibility had led Origen to maintain that the generation of the Son by the Father did not lead to any change in God (see above, p. 168), and Tertullian had argued that only the human nature in Jesus suffered, not the divine. Nestorius now applied the doctrine of impassibility much more rigorously, to support the view that in Jesus there must be not only two complete natures, divine and human, but two distinct individuals *(hypostases),* one of whom, the human Jesus, is the subject of Jesus' human experiences and actions, the other, the indwelling divine Word, the one who performs his divine actions such as working miracles and seeing into people's hearts.

Nestorius criticized ways of speaking about Jesus which confused his human and divine actions and experiences. One term summed up his fears — the title *Theotokos* (meaning, 'who gave birth to God' or, traditionally, 'Mother of God') which was sometimes applied to the Virgin Mary. In Nestorius' view to say that Mary gave birth to God was clearly to confuse Jesus' divine and human natures. Mary gave birth only to the humanity of Christ.

Cyril of Alexandria

Nestorius' view was not put forward with any desire to promote a new doctrine, but simply as a drawing out of the logical consequences of rejecting Arianism and Apollinarianism and maintaining that Jesus was fully divine and fully human. But Nestorius aroused the hostility of Cyril, Bishop of Alexandria, who in a series of sermons and letters attacked him for teaching a doctrine of 'two Sons' and even of worshipping the human and divine natures of Jesus as if they were separate *(Second Letter to Nestorius; Creeds, Councils and Controversies,* pp. 295-97). He rejected Nestorius' view that speaking of Christ as a single 'person' *(prosopon,* not *hypostasis,* in Greek) was an adequate safeguard of his unity, since Nestorius in fact divided Jesus' actions and experiences between the two natures.

Cyril's own view of the person of Jesus was based on the creed of Nicaea and his interpretation of John 1.14 ('The Word became flesh'). Neither the creed nor John spoke of Jesus as a human being separate from the divine Logos, but of the Logos taking human flesh (and soul: John 1.14 had to be interpreted so as to exclude Apollinarianism) and making it his own:

> The Word, having in an ineffable and inconceivable manner personally united to himself flesh animated with living soul, became man and was called Son of Man, yet not of mere will or favour, nor

again by the simple assumption to himself of a human person. (*Second Letter to Nestorius; Creeds, Councils and Controversies*, p. 296)

From Cyril's point of view, it was clear that the union of Word and flesh in Jesus was a union of *hypostasis* or even of nature (an idea which Cyril borrowed, probably without realizing its heretical origin, from Apollinaris); there is only one individual being, Jesus, who is both divine and human, so that all of Jesus' actions and experiences, human and divine, have the same subject.

It is at this point that Cyril's theology becomes more complicated. Cyril wanted to say that Jesus' human experiences such as fear or suffering all belonged to the divine Word in the same way as his divine qualities. This included the experience of human birth: for Cyril it was essential to say that Mary is *Theotokos*.

But this was difficult without appearing to deny the doctrine of God's impassibility — as Nestorius had realized. So Cyril argued that the Word suffered not in his own nature but only in so far as the body which suffered them belonged to the Word himself, not to a human Jesus considered separately (*Creeds, Councils and Controversies*, p. 296). The incarnation thus marks a real union of divine and human life, the divine Word willingly associating himself with and experiencing what it is to be a human being. Using the language of Philippians 2, Cyril spoke about the incarnation as an act of 'self-emptying' *(kenosis)* or the assumption of 'the form of a servant' by the Word (cf. Bettenson, *The Later Christian Fathers*, p. 261).

It is a serious question, whether it is possible to make sense of the doctrine that the Word suffers, yet not in his own nature, but in his own flesh. Cyril stressed that the union of humanity and divinity was something incomprehensible to the human mind, therefore something which we should expect to have difficulty expressing without recourse to paradox. But the question remains, whether defining the suffering and mental limitations (such as ignorance) of Jesus as belonging to the Word, not to a human Jesus, is to risk making them unreal because the Word cannot really experience them — Cyril's theology is not free of traces of docetism.

Nevertheless, Cyril deserves notice for taking the bold step of wanting to say, in however qualified a sense, that 'the Word suffered' in Jesus or even 'the Word tasted death' (Cyril, *Twelve Anathemas against*

Nestorius; Creeds, Councils and Controversies, p. 308). Ignatius had made one similar remark (see the beginning of this chapter), but, in view of the development of the doctrine of divine impassibility since the third century, it is remarkable that Cyril should have done so. His willingness to stretch the doctrine of impassibility to breaking point in this way makes him, among the Church fathers, the strongest proponent of the doctrine that in Jesus, the Son of God really identified himself with the human condition.

The Councils of Ephesus and Chalcedon

Like the Arian controversy a century before, the dispute between Cyril and Nestorius could only be resolved by a council of bishops. This met at Ephesus in June 431 (the third ecumenical council) and the teaching of Nestorius was condemned. Cyril, however, faced criticism from a number of bishops because of his insistence on saying that the Word suffered in his *Twelve Anathemas against Nestorius* (referred to above). Cyril was eventually forced into an agreement with John, Bishop of Antioch (the leader of the opposition to Cyril after Nestorius had been condemned). This agreement is known as the Formula of Reunion (see *Creeds, Councils and Controversies*, pp. 313-17); it makes no reference to Cyril's controversial teaching, and clearly explains that the human and divine actions and experiences of Jesus each belong to the appropriate nature, so the human experiences are not ascribed to the Word.

Following Nestorius' condemnation and Cyril's compromise (and death in 444) it must have seemed as if the controversy was over; but the Church still lacked a formula which commanded general agreement to define the relationship of the human and divine in Jesus. The stimulus to produce such a formula was a further period of dispute between an Alexandrian bishop (Dioscorus) and his rival in Constantinople (Flavian). What was achieved when the Council of Chalcedon (the fourth ecumenical council) met to resolve the controversy in October 451 was a doctrinal statement around which the vast majority of bishops could unite — the exceptions being supporters of Dioscorus from Egypt and Palestine, who regarded any statement which referred to Christ as 'two natures' as Nestorian.

Like the creeds of Nicaea and Constantinople, the definition of faith of Chalcedon (as it is called) must be quoted in full.

The Definition of Chalcedon

Following the holy fathers, we all with one voice confess our Lord Jesus Christ one and the same Son, the same perfect in Godhead, the same perfect in manhood, truly God and truly man, the same consisting of a reasonable soul and a body, of one substance with the Father as touching the Godhead, the same of one substance with us as touching the manhood, 'like us in all things apart from sin' [Heb. 4.15]; begotten of the Father before the ages as touching the Godhead, the same in the last days, for us and for our salvation, born from the Virgin Mary, the *Theotokos*, as touching the manhood, one and same Christ, Son, Lord, Only-begotten, to be acknowledged in two natures, without confusion, without change, without division, without separation; the distinction of natures being in no way abolished because of the union, but rather the characteristic property of each nature being preserved, and concurring into one person and one *hypostasis*, not as if Christ were parted or divided into two persons, but one and the same Son and only-begotten God, Word, Lord, Jesus Christ.

(*Creeds, Councils and Controversies*, pp. 352-53)

Much of the definition is concerned with establishing the reality of Christ's human and divine natures; the repeated use of the phrase 'the same' shows, however, that these natures are not conceived of as belonging to the human Jesus and the indwelling divine Word separately, but to one individual, who is both Word and human, born first of God and then of Mary, the *Theotokos*.

In this way, Cyril's emphasis on the unity of Christ is respected (the inclusion of the term *Theotokos* shows a clear preference for his views over those of Nestorius); however, the definition insists that Jesus is 'in two natures' and that these natures, divine and human, are not changed or confused by the incarnation — as Cyril's teaching on the suffering of the Word was held by many to imply. On the other hand again, the unity of person and *hypostasis* taught by the definition would have been acceptable to Cyril.

Continued Debate

Despite the success of the Council of Chalcedon in the context of a Church which was weary of controversy, a century was to elapse before the terms of the definition of Chalcedon were finally accepted in the Church in the Roman empire (and its successor in the Eastern Mediterranean and Middle East, the Byzantine empire). Even then, agreement on the terms of the definition — which still unites the Eastern Orthodox, Catholic, and Protestant churches — was at the cost of permanent schism in Syria and Egypt; the Syrian Orthodox and Coptic churches (among others) of today are defined by their rejection of Chalcedon and its 'in two natures' formula.

Among modern theologians too there is continued debate about the interpretation of the definition of Chalcedon. Does the reference to one *hypostasis* (and the *Theotokos*) imply Cyril's view that Jesus' human experiences are the experiences of the Word, so that someone who accepts the definition can say (with Cyril) that God suffered or even that he died on the cross? Since many Christians today question the value to theology of Greek philosophical ideas such as the doctrine of divine impassibility (accepted by all the participants in the fifth-century debate, though in Cyril's case perhaps with some reluctance) this is an important question which bears on whether or not the definition has a continuing positive value for modern theology.

Because questions like this are hard to answer, the view is quite common that Chalcedon should be regarded as essentially a negative statement (the exclusion on the one hand of Nestorianism and on the other of Apollinarianism and docetism) rather than a positive doctrinal achievement like the creeds of Nicaea and Constantinople. Perhaps it should be seen not as an attempt to explain the union of Word and humanity in Jesus but simply as a definition of the problem. But, as a summary of early Christian teaching on the incarnation the definition remains important from the point of view of what constitutes orthodox Christianity. No one can be regarded as a heretic who holds to the traditional doctrines of the Trinity and the incarnation as defined at Nicaea and Chalcedon; modern theology, on the other hand, may be judged by whether it is as successful as the traditional doctrines in preserving and conveying the New Testament message of Jesus as the Son of God and bringer of salvation.

Modern Understandings of Jesus

As we saw in Chapter 1, the doctrines of the Trinity and the incarnation which emerged during the first four centuries of Christianity went almost unchallenged for over a thousand years. Not until the sixteenth century were they subjected to any real criticism, with the development in Europe of a movement called Socinianism, after an Italian theologian, F. P. Sozzini (1539-1604). The term 'Socinian' continued to be applied to Unitarians — i.e., to Christians who rejected the doctrine of the Trinity — until the nineteenth century.

> **Unitarianism**: a form of Christian belief with roots in the sixteenth century, which denies the doctrine of the Trinity and the divinity of Jesus, often on the grounds that they are not taught explicitly in the New Testament. In the late eighteenth century Unitarianism emerged as a distinct Christian denomination in Britain and America. Most unitarians are also universalists, believing either that all human beings will be saved, or at least that salvation may be obtained by faithful following of many religious traditions, not just Christianity.

But Socinian views remained the preserve of a small minority of Christians who were often isolated from the mainstream of theological development represented by Protestant and Catholic thought; it was not until the eighteenth century, under the influence of the European Enlightenment, that a number of theologians in the larger churches began to develop liberal or radical views which questioned the traditional Christian beliefs about Jesus.

Liberal Views since the Enlightenment

The Nature of the Enlightenment

The Enlightenment was, in part, a reaction against Greco-Roman (or ancient) philosophy, exemplified by Plato and Aristotle, and it had enormous consequences for Christian doctrine partly because of the use which Christian theologians had made of philosophy in articulating their views. Ancient philosophy was a huge intellectual achievement. It was devoted to setting out rational criteria for criticizing arguments and opinions (logic), developing an understanding of the nature of the universe (physics), and mapping the proper way for human beings to live in accordance with their own nature and true beliefs (ethics). But ancient philosophy and the use to which it had been put to support Christian doctrine, both in the early Church and in the Middle Ages in the work of theologians such as Thomas Aquinas (1225-74), had come to look like a dead end to many eighteenth-century intellectuals.

Science and History

Where ancient philosophy was weak was in its scientific understanding of the universe and its understanding of history. Since the seventeenth century (when the scientific views of Aristotle were finally abandoned), science had both discovered many new laws about the physical universe but also come to appreciate that far more remained to be discovered than was already known. To philosophers, it began to look as if Plato's or Aristotle's ability to explain the universe was limited by a lack of scientific knowledge; it was implausible to suggest that a definitive account of the world could be given in terms of concepts drawn from ancient philosophy or speculations based on them, such as the arguments of Christian theologians about the divine Logos as creator of the world. Philosophy became more sceptical and empirical and rejected any explanation of the universe which did not conform to established scientific beliefs.

Scepticism: the belief that complete knowledge of the world, particularly its nature and causes, is unattainable; against the view — typical of ancient philosophy — that the human mind is able to understand the world by the application of pure reason. Scepticism originated in the Greco-Roman world, but did not become common until the eighteenth century.

Empiricism: the belief that philosophy should confine itself to describing what can be known through observation or scientific study, and that beliefs about the nature of the world should not be based on postulating the existence of any higher principle, such as God, whose existence cannot be proved.

This trend in philosophy is exemplified by the Scottish philosopher David Hume (1711-76), who is well known for his rejection of miracles, and more generally for his denial that God could be known to be the cause of any event — because events could only be described in terms of scientific laws derived from observation, not explained.

The second area of weakness of ancient philosophy, history, was equally important. Ancient philosophy had typically sought to understand the world and to assess human conduct in terms of conformity to a 'nature' regarded as universal and permanent. The Enlightenment changed this: the historical evolution of societies and cultures and the differences between them began to be understood, partly assisted by greater knowledge of non-European societies and ethical and religious systems. It was not so necessary to see history and societies as governed by God: they could have their own, inherent principles of development, morality, and justice, and did not need to have these imposed on them from outside, either by God or by an abstract philosophical system. The development of economics from a branch of ethics (in which right behaviour was prescribed by external standards — God or justice) into an empirical science intended to describe and understand human behaviour in the context of a particular economic or social system is a good illustration of the Enlightenment intellectual revolution.

Historical empiricism was also applied to Christian beliefs. It was no longer sufficient to believe doctrines such as the Trinity and the incarnation because they were logically coherent in themselves (assuming that they were), because they were traditional, or because they were taught in authoritative sources such as Scripture, interpreted in a way unchanged for centuries. The development of ideas was studied, and it was realized that later ideas did not necessarily follow from earlier ones — the doctrine of the *homoousios* as taught by Athanasius, for example, did not develop inevitably from the ideas of Justin about the Logos. Indeed, there might be a considerable difference between the two doctrines, which conventional ways of looking at the early Church as part of an unbroken tradition of self-consistent theological teaching tended to conceal.

Theological Consequences of the Enlightenment

For theologians, the Enlightenment was a challenge. Not all theologians, of course, responded by abandoning the traditional doctrines about Jesus. They adopted commonly accepted (Enlightenment) principles of empirical observation, practical reason, and historical criticism in an attempt to provide a more secure foundation for their beliefs than ancient philosophical arguments and to ensure that they conformed to what could be known historically about the figure of Jesus and the doctrines of the early Church. This is essentially what Newton and Whiston (see Chapter 1) attempted to do, but it could have unexpected and unwelcome consequences if, as in their case, the historical study of the Bible and the early Church actually led theologians to find that the traditional doctrines about Jesus were inadequately supported by the evidence.

One way of coping with doubts about whether the traditional doctrines were historically well founded was to adopt a less dogmatically ambitious approach than traditional Christian thought. Perhaps Christian belief had invested too much intellectual energy in the attempt to define God as a Trinity consisting of three persons who are united in a single substance, or the figure of Jesus as one person existing in two natures. If it was possible to step back from these doctrinal formulations and to accept a less precise, even a deliberately vague or ambiguous, understanding of the relationship of Jesus to God, there might be less danger of the foundations of Christian belief being undermined. If Christian beliefs about Jesus are to be based on the historical evidence of the New Testament, it may be wise to accept that there are things about him which are uncertain and not susceptible to historical proof, and to be in less of a hurry to express beliefs based on uncertain empirical evidence in exact, philosophical language.

Many of the best-known attempts to reinterpret Christian belief in the course of the eighteenth and nineteenth centuries may be understood in the light of this observation. For example, the German theologian F. D. E. Schleiermacher (1768-1834) reacted against both the traditional dogmatic theology of his day and the hostility of many Enlightenment thinkers to religious belief. Schleiermacher attempted to base Christian belief on an intuition or feeling of dependence on God, which was exemplified to the fullest extent in the life of Jesus. Christianity could not be defended against Enlightenment criticism by appealing directly to the reasonableness of doctrines such as the Trinity and the incarnation, but only by means of ideas which made sense both of Jesus' human life (in so far as its reality can be discovered by biblical scholarship) and the experience of believers today.

Mystery

In some ways the less dogmatically ambitious approach to theology of many post-Enlightenment theologians is in agreement with a much older insight of the Christian tradition, that there is an element of mystery or of uncertainty in our understanding of God and of the figure of Jesus. Early Christian theologians were aware that the doctrines of the Trinity and the incarnation appear paradoxical to unaided human reason, but they believed that intellectual humility was called for in the face of the unimaginable greatness of God's being, which is far beyond human ability to comprehend. Liberal theology, as represented by Schleiermacher, simply puts this insight into practice by refraining from dogmatism in areas where earlier Christian theologians had not feared to tread.

Not all theologians since the eighteenth century have been happy with the loss of both dogmatic and historical certainty which this approach to theology implies, but many have felt there is no alternative but to adopt it — particularly in view of the doubts raised by biblical scholarship about the historical reliability of the Gospel portrayal of Jesus. In the rest of this section we will look (in rather general terms) at some of the ways in which liberal theologians have sought to reinterpret the doctrines of the Trinity and the incarnation.

God as Trinity

Explicit abandonment of belief in the Trinity has always been a minority response to the Enlightenment criticism of traditional doctrine, but reconstruction or reinterpretation of the doctrine has been much more common. Most liberal theologians would agree that Christian belief requires talk of a Trinity of Father, Son, and Holy Spirit, which is what the New Testament witness points to, and what the whole development of early Christian theology and the pattern of Christian worship and devotion to the figure of Jesus through the centuries have been based on. One cannot abandon a belief like the Trinity easily and still claim to belong to the religious tradition which formulated it. But whether belief in the Trinity has to be expressed in the precise dogmatic constructions developed by the early Church is another question.

A Non-dogmatic Trinity

Early Christian theology sought to answer the question, exactly how is God as Trinity to be understood? The answer was in the philosophical language of substance and person. Liberal theology might be content with answering the less dogmatic question, what characteristics of God does talking about him in Trinitarian terms help us to understand? For example, belief in the Trinity expresses the character of God as love, and of the world which he has created as one in which personal relationships, modelled on the idea of a divine family united by love, are at the heart of what it is to be fully human. Theology can teach that God is love, that he reveals his love most fully and perfectly in Jesus, and that the universe takes its character from the fact that its creator is one who wishes to share his love with a Son, without necessarily wanting to go

193

further and to define Jesus as a divine person identical with the Father in substance (that is, using an ancient philosophical understanding of 'substance', as a being who shares exactly the same qualities or attributes, such as perfect goodness, power, and knowledge, as the Father).

Or maybe talking about God as Father, Son, and Holy Spirit should be seen primarily as a way of pointing out the different ways in which Christians respond to God. For example, to talk about God as Father implies responding to him as creator, as the one who holds all things in his power, who embraces all things in his love and cares for all things equally. To talk about God as Son or as Jesus emphasizes the more personal aspect of our relationship to God, since Jesus is the one to whom Christians respond in a life dedicated to God, whose example of prayer and service to others they follow. To talk about God as Spirit emphasizes the character of God as active, living, and energizing, the source of everything that is good and holy in the way Christians worship and the way they live their lives. The embedding of the Trinity in the language of Christian worship and spirituality ensures that all these aspects of Christians' relationship to God are held together. Christians can believe that all of these aspects of God (creator, personal saviour, active presence) are genuinely reflected in his being and in his relationship with Jesus, without committing themselves to using the dogmatic language of the early Church.

So there are ways of thinking about the Trinity different from the strongly philosophical, dogmatic way, which the ancient Church developed. This is not to say that Christians cannot engage in some doctrinal construction, just that there are reasons why post-Enlightenment theologians of a liberal disposition have wanted to modify the traditional doctrinal position. Liberal theologians may continue to use the language of God as Trinity (though some have practically abandoned it), but will want to consider what this language implies (what its role is in Christian life and worship) and what can reasonably be said on the basis of it about God and our experience of him, rather than constructing a strictly defined Trinitarian dogma such as the 'three persons in one substance' of the early Church.

Jesus as Divine and Human

Liberal theology wishes to express certain insights into the nature of God, such as his creation of a world where loving relationships are central to human flourishing, but without committing itself to a doctrine of God expressed in over-precise philosophical terms. This can be done while retaining a commitment to the belief that Jesus is divine — in the sense that his human life is the clearest and fullest revelation to human beings of the nature of God, and therefore embodies (or incarnates) and presents God to the world. If we are to go any further than this in an assessment of the person of Jesus, we come up against difficult historical and conceptual questions: what is the historical basis for believing that Jesus was divine, and does the notion of an incarnation — as the Church fathers would have understood that term — make sense outside their philosophical framework?

The Historical Basis

To modern eyes, it is almost inevitable that theologians of the early Church will appear to have read Scripture in a very naïve way when they took it as evidence that Jesus was a divine person become human. They took what to us seem like very vague hints in the Old Testament about the figure of the Messiah, or the figure of Wisdom (see p. 71) — a personified quality of God in the Old Testament (notably the book of Proverbs) — and interpreted these as evidence that the Old Testament authors actually foresaw, in considerable detail, the life, death, and resurrection of Jesus. Alongside this prophetic proof of Jesus' status as God's Son or Messiah (which is expounded, for example, in the works of Justin and Origen) the Church fathers set a range information about him — his miracles, his teaching, his authority over demons, and his power to forgive sins — and erected it into what to them was very clear proof that he was a divine being. Even then they were not finished, for they took New Testament hints about Jesus' pre-existence (e.g., Col. 1.15 and John 1.1) and developed them, with the aid of the Logos-doctrine of Middle Platonist philosophy, into the fully-fledged doctrine of Jesus as God's creative Logos, which in the second century became the basis of the doctrines of the Trinity and incarnation.

Modern readers of the Bible know much more than writers of the early Church could possibly have done about the type of literature that is contained in the Bible, about the nature of metaphor, about the way in which beliefs about the Messiah accumulated, and the way in which Christian beliefs about Jesus developed over time, including within the period of the New Testament itself. We are aware of how the New Testament presentation of Jesus was shaped by beliefs about him, so that it cannot be used as purely objective historical evidence for his life and status. For example, we know that some of the Gospel statements that Jesus fulfilled prophecy — and the events in his life that are alleged to have done so — were probably created in the light of the belief that he was the Messiah, and cannot be used as evidence to support the belief (e.g., the story of Jesus' flight into Egypt — Matt. 2.13-15).

Unless modern Christians are going to pretend that they live in the second or fourth century, and to take Scripture exactly as it was taken by the tradition prior to the Enlightenment, it is difficult to accept that there is as much historical basis in Scripture for believing that Jesus was divine as the early Church commonly thought. For this reason alone, the liberal project of refusing to be too dogmatic about claiming that Jesus was divine seems amply justified.

The Two Natures

As has been noted above, the Church fathers were happy to accept that belief in the incarnation involved accepting something paradoxical. Cyril of Alexandria, who believed that in the incarnation the Word of God suffered in the flesh, constantly underlines that the incarnation is incomprehensible and inexpressible. But liberal theologians will want to ask the question, is it possible to spell out what it means to say that Jesus is God incarnate at all, even allowing for an element of paradox? Cyril was an outstanding Christian thinker who had a profound grasp of what was involved in the idea of incarnation, the idea of God in Jesus identifying himself with human experiences and human limitations in such a way that the life of Jesus is perceived by people as redemptive, as providing them with hope, a sense that human life can be redeemed. That is a very important theological insight. Nevertheless, the question remains, can Cyril's view be made plausible, so that it can be held as a reasonable belief about the historical figure of Jesus? How much sense does it make to say that Jesus as he appears in the Gospels, a human being who genuinely suffered and died on the cross, was also a divine being?

This is a very difficult question to answer, even more so when it is put in technical terms and we ask, in the language of the definition of Chalcedon, what does it actually mean to say that Jesus is one person 'in two natures'? If the idea cannot be spelt out in coherent terms — and it is certainly difficult to do so — then perhaps the viewpoint which was referred to at the end of Chapter 8, that Chalcedon was essentially a negative achievement, successful at excluding certain beliefs, rather than a positive one, is correct.

Radical Views

The difficulty of believing in the Chalcedonian doctrine of two natures and thus of making good sense of the idea of the incarnation as it has traditionally been understood has certainly been among the main reasons for rejecting the belief that Jesus was both divine and human. Some theologians have argued that it is possible for Christianity to do without Jesus as a divine figure, to see him simply as a moral teacher or the supreme example of someone who lived out a life of complete self-dedication to the purposes of God.

This has the advantage of helping to preserve the centrality of Jesus to the Christian faith, even though some of Jesus' own teachings and beliefs were mistaken — for example, his expectation of a quick and sudden end of the world following his ministry. (The failure of Jesus' prophecies of the end of the world to be fulfilled certainly poses a problem for the traditional view of Jesus, since, as God, he should have known everything that the Father knew — as the traditional doctrine of the incarnation teaches.) Some theologians such as Rudolf Bultmann (see Chapter 1) have even argued that Christianity should abandon not only any dogmatic claims about Jesus' divine nature, but all except a few minimal historical claims about him, in the interests of seeing his religious significance not in any facts about his person, but in the challenge to dedicate ourselves to God presented to us by the 'Christ of faith' or the 'Christ event' proclaimed by the New Testament authors.

Radicalism is not, however, the way that the majority of Christian theologians have been happy to regard Jesus, even if they are influenced by the concerns of the Enlightenment. On the whole, liberal theology has tried to preserve the belief that in the historical figure of Jesus, God revealed himself to human beings and brought a new salvation based on a better and fuller knowledge of God and his purposes than was available before. The historical Jesus and the traditional doctrines about him remain of significance for liberal theology, even though a question mark is placed against the historical evidence on the basis of which the early Church sought to prove Jesus' divinity, and the terms in which it sought to define it.

Conservative Reactions

The influence of liberal theology grew during the nineteenth and much of the twentieth centuries, at least in university theology and often in the mainstream churches (Protestant if not Catholic) as well. However, liberalism has not had matters all its own way. Conservative commitment to the doctrines of the early Christian creeds and the authority of Scripture as traditionally interpreted remained a force, and underwent a renewal in the twentieth century through the work of Karl Barth (see Chapter 1) and his successors, particularly in Britain and the United States.

The Present Situation

Because of the new-found confidence of conservative theology, recent theology has been strongly polarized between those who wish to continue the pursuit of a liberal theological agenda, and those who have developed a conservative response to Enlightenment criticism of traditional doctrines. Liberals typically try to incorporate new areas of enquiry into their critique of traditional Christian doctrines, asking questions about their validity from new points of view represented by feminists, political radicals, and liberation, green, gay and lesbian theologians, and other groups who want to bring their understanding of Jesus into relation with their own contextual theological agenda.

Conservatives, on the other hand, while sometimes distinctly hostile to trends such as feminist or green theology (which can be associated, from a traditional Christian point of view, with a questioning of

> **Contextual theology**: an understanding that the questions theologians ask will vary according to their context — their position in life including their gender, ethnic group, class, sexual orientation, and so on — so that (for example) theology done among the poor or those excluded from consumer society should reflect their particular experience and viewpoint.

the central place of humanity in God's purpose in creating a world), have been able to point to a number of trends in recent philosophy which are more favourable to traditional Christian teaching than the empiricism of the Enlightenment. In the last fifteen years or so the movement known as postmodernism has given a new lease of life to conservative theologies by placing a question mark against the claims of the Enlightenment to supply objective, empirical criticisms of Christian doctrine.

> **Postmodernism**: a complex phenomenon in modern philosophy and culture, the basis of which is the questioning of the capacity of human beings to form objective opinions about facts and situations. All knowledge is relative and subjective (i.e., not universally valid) and constructed (i.e., created by the one who knows, not received from the world about us). Postmodernism rejects both the dogmatism of ancient philosophy and the scientific empiricism of the Enlightenment in favour of a flexible, constantly changing mental outlook. Postmodernism has been adopted by both liberal and conservative theologians, though is probably more influential among the latter.

If all thought is valid only in the context in which it is uttered, then the construction of doctrines such as the Trinity and the incarnation by Christians attempting to live out their faith in the context of a worshipping community following the teaching of the Bible has a validity in its own terms which cannot be undermined simply by the Enlightenment attempt to show that not all of the Church's doctrines make logical or historical sense.

The success of the revival of orthodox theology led by Karl Barth and the rise of postmodernism have led many conservative theologians to speak of the death of liberal theology or even the end of the Enlightenment. While such opinions are clearly exaggerated, conservatism, in both its Barthian and postmodern forms, has dominated university theology in Britain and the United States in the last decade or so. (A leading representative of the Barthian tradition was Professor Colin Gunton (1941-2003) of King's College London.) But modern conservatism looks very different from the tradition of theology which prevailed before the Enlightenment, not least because modern conservatives have generally taken on board the Enlightenment view that traditional Christian beliefs cannot be built up on the basis of reason and evidence alone, or tied to the acceptance of a particular philosophical terminology such as that of the Greco-Roman world. Modern conservative theology prefers to seek support for its position in tradition (understood in a new way), imagination (a force not to be underestimated in theology), and above all in revelation.

Conservative Emphases

Tradition

Conservatives — even Protestants who for most of their existence have been hostile to the idea that tradition should have a decisive role in how Christian doctrine is formulated — in recent times have become much more convinced of the importance of tradition. According to this outlook, while, viewed from the point of view of Enlightenment criticism, it cannot be taken for granted that the New Testament consistently teaches that Jesus is God, or that the Old Testament image of Wisdom provides us with supporting evidence for the idea of God as Trinity, nevertheless Christians should continue to use the Bible in this way, simply because this is the way the Bible has been used within Christian reflection and Christian worship for hundreds of years.

An intellectually creative tradition such as Christianity, which has produced new theological ideas throughout its history, which has inspired human beings to many acts of goodness and heroic self-sacrifice, has created or inspired all kinds of works of art and literature, and has nourished the spiritual lives of countless people — a tradition like that has a validity in itself, and Christians should continue to affirm it.

Conservatives are not unaware of the problems of believing in Jesus' divinity on the basis of the evidence, but they argue that Christians would need extremely good reasons for abandoning the theological positions of two millennia, and that the Enlightenment has not provided such convincing reasons. It is to some degree legitimate to compartmentalize: to say, when working as a Christian theologian, that theologians can continue to work within the tradition and do not have to take notice immediately of what everyone outside it may be saying. A tradition that is worthy of being lived, or being worked through intellectually and spiritually, will prove its worth. In a way it can fight its own battles.

Imagination

It would probably be true to say that both conservative and liberal theologians in recent years have paid increasing attention to the role of imagination in theology, partly as a result of the decline of confidence in the ability of philosophy (whether traditional or Enlightenment) and science to provide intellectual support for religious beliefs. In particular, theology has emphasized the idea of Christian doctrine, not as abstract philosophical construction but as story — a story about God and his interaction with the world, finding its central narrative moment in the figure of Jesus and the New Testament accounts of the earliest Christians' experience of him as risen Lord.

The notion of Christian doctrine as telling a story about the relationship between God and human beings is an appeal to imagination and the capacity for intelligent, creative spiritual interaction with the words of Scripture, even though we know that not all of it is true in every historical detail, because we think they tell us something significant about our own condition and the world in which we live. The scriptural story, in other words, makes sense because it relates to our story.

Theology as story or narrative has the capability to transcend Enlightenment scepticism about the historical Jesus or the possibility of miracles, which are such a stumbling block to many people's understanding of the message of Scripture if it is taken literally, and return to the Bible some of its power to transform human lives. Perhaps also, narrative theology (or imaginative theology generally) has the capability to transcend the differences between liberal and conservative theologians — and there are indeed signs in recent years that some of their disagreements may well be becoming less heated. (The popularity in contemporary theology of the work of the Archbishop of Canterbury, Rowan Williams, is partly due to his appeal to imagination, story, and mystery in his writings, and his ability to make the message of Scripture contemporary and challenging in a way that grips both liberal and conservative readers.)

Revelation

Nonetheless, the centre of the modern conservative revival in theology remains not merely a commitment to church tradition or an imaginative response to Scripture, but a belief in divine revelation, communicated to human beings in the words of Scripture and in the life and person of Jesus which Scripture mediates to us. As we have seen in Chapter 1, Karl Barth's theology was built on the concept of the Word of God as a purely biblical notion, unencumbered by the philosophical connotations with which early Christian theologians invested it. Modern conservatism has followed through Barth's insight, retaining his commitment to the whole of Scripture as a means of divine revelation, but often also broadening it to embrace the belief that the doctrinal structures which Christianity has inherited from the early Church, the Middle Ages, and (for Protestants) also from the sixteenth-century Reformation are themselves validated by God's continuing guidance of the Church through the action of his Holy Spirit, the divine presence at work in all Christian life. (Pneumatology — the doctrine of the Holy Spirit — has been a particularly important emphasis in modern conservative theology.)

If something is revealed by God, then the degree to which it may be subject to valid criticism by merely human minds may well be limited. Human beings are asked to respond to revelation in humility, and accept the guidance of their thoughts by the Bible and tradition. In so far as revelation can be understood as making available to human beings knowledge of God which can be expressed in theological doctrines (a view of revelation which many liberals, naturally, would reject, since they are inclined to see Christian doctrine as a human response to revelation, rather than as part of it), belief in revelation helps Christians to think that the tradition in which they live has a validity that goes beyond whatever merely logical appeal there may be in its ideas.

Where Is Jesus in It All Today?

The Crucial Question

Where does Jesus stand amid all this doctrinal reconstruction? Perhaps as an amused bystander, since admittedly a lot of what passes for Christology or doctrinal teaching about Jesus in modern theology seems to make little reference to the Jesus of the Gospels. If early Christian doctrine sometimes seems to focus on the more abstract features of the doctrines of the Trinity and the incarnation to the neglect of the person of Jesus, then the Enlightenment has not always succeeded in transferring attention away from concern with the idea of Jesus — concepts of his nature and person — and back to the historical figure we read about in the Gospels.

Biblical scholarship must take some of the blame for this neglect, for sometimes in the wake of the Enlightenment it became so sceptical about what may be known about the figure of Jesus, that it lost sight of the (perfectly valid) task of making his life and message understood in terms that modern Christians can easily relate to.

But neither has the renewed conservatism restored the focus of theology to the figure of Jesus; both liberal and conservative theology as practised at the present time still tend to centre their debates on philosophical arguments — given renewed impetus by the growth of postmodern scepticism about all philosophical knowledge — rather than asking the only ultimately vital questions about Jesus — how much can we really know about him as a historical figure, and what is his significance for us?

A theologian — whether traditional or modern — may be able to produce a coherent explanation of how Jesus could be both a human and a divine person, or how he could be said to be God and yet suffer and die; but how are Christians today to know that this account is true? From the point of view of many Christians who want to follow Jesus' teaching and take him as a guide to the character of God, debates about the doctrine of divine impassibility (see Chapter 8) or about whether Jesus was all-knowing or perfectly good make comparatively little sense if we do not have adequate evidence from the Gospels to guide us in thinking about them. Even though modern conservative theology commands respect for its emphasis on tradition and imagination, we probably have to admit, with the liberals of the eighteenth and nineteenth centuries, that the validity of the traditional doctrines about Jesus is something that, on the basis of the Gospel evidence, we will never be able to establish.

Fortunately, as readers of earlier chapters of this book will know, modern biblical scholarship has renewed its attention to the historical figure of Jesus, and in terms of accessible accounts of who he was and what we can know about him, modern Christians (and enquirers from other religious traditions and none) are in a much better position than some of their predecessors to answer for themselves the question of his importance.

What Should Christians Believe about Jesus?

'A Kind and Generous Man'

At the very least, it is important for contemporary Christians to be able to know that Jesus was a good man who showed his care for others by his actions and his words, who in his own life set an example of the moral goodness which he taught. To take a very simple example: Jesus told tax collectors and sinners that God loved them, and he showed this love in action by the way in which he himself behaved towards them, which showed them that they too (not just righteous people) would be included in the Kingdom of God.

The importance of believing that Jesus was a good man is affirmed by E. P. Sanders in his important book *The Historical Figure of Jesus* (Harmondsworth: Penguin, 1993). Sanders is by no means concerned to show that the Gospel evidence is a completely accurate portrait of the historical Jesus: the early Church has contributed a lot of material to the Gospels which does not go back to Jesus himself. Nevertheless he thinks it possible, on the basis of the clear evidence of how Jesus behaved throughout his life, to predict the way in which he would have behaved in moral or ethical situations where the evidence of the Gospels is a bit less clear. For instance, we can say on the basis of the fact that Jesus was 'a kind and generous man' (p. 192), that he probably did anticipate the inclusion of some non-Jews in the Kingdom of God, since the alternative would be the (less generous) one of believing in their destruction, even though the Gospel evidence that teaching to this effect was a feature of Jesus' ministry (as opposed to the viewpoint of the early Church) is fairly slight.

Unless Christians can say things like that about Jesus with relative certainty, there is no secure basis for Christian faith as having anything to do with the historical figure of Jesus, and it would be very difficult for Christianity in anything like its traditional forms to continue. This is not simply another reference to the problems of believing the traditional doctrines about Jesus: in this case, the reference is to the much broader picture of Christian worship, spirituality, and ethics, in so far as these are closely linked to the figure of Jesus in the Gospels. Although it was the resurrection which brought the Christian movement into being, the character of Jesus has been an inspiration for Christians throughout the centuries; unless we can be sure that the historical Jesus did resemble the figure of the Gospels, it is hard to see how a religion centred on his death and resurrection could be credible.

Liberal Christians may be able to accept a Jesus who was wrong about the imminent end of the world (see above, p. 197), but a Jesus who was discovered by historical investigation to have been a racist, or whose teaching was flawed by intolerance or lack of sympathy with his fellow human beings, could not be explained away by the Christian religion.

A Morally Flawed Jesus?

Some theologians have thought that a Jesus who suffered from some of these moral defects might still be a credible saviour figure, in that the doctrine of the incarnation involves the idea of God becoming a human being; that particular human being, the argument goes, could have turned out to be morally flawed in certain ways but could still have been used by God for his saving purposes. Sometimes this idea may be of use in biblical interpretation — for example to explain the incident (Mark

7.25-30) where Jesus uses language to a Greek woman which comes close to referring to her as a dog.

This is certainly a difficult saying of Jesus to understand (though read in its proper historical context in Jesus' ministry the superficial suggestion of racism is much less forceful). But the solution proposed does not seem credible, precisely because it seems to require an *initial* commitment to the idea of incarnation, and only then the application of the idea to the figure of Jesus. It implies that doctrines such as that Jesus was the second person of the Trinity come to earth are much more important than what he was actually like. It invests too much in the ideas, and not enough in what we see about the facts. This leaves it open, in the end, to the liberal criticism that it is an arbitrary doctrinal construction that is simply not credible. So it is important that Christians can be sure of the character of Jesus, if he is to serve as a moral teacher and an example for Christians.

Jesus and Contemporary Theological Dilemmas

This emphasis on what Jesus was actually like as a historical individual is not meant to preclude Christians from viewing Jesus as a political liberal, a radical, a feminist, or a green, if they wish to. However, reconstructions which place a lot of emphasis on a Jesus of this sort (say, a feminist Jesus, one of whose main aims in his ministry was to affirm women and undermine the patriarchal outlook of his culture) do go beyond what we can reasonably say on the basis of the Gospel material. This is not to say that they are invalid, only that they are not historical descriptions. Many Christians have found strength and inspiration in speculating about what Jesus would have done, if he were exercising his ministry in the context that they find themselves in: and there is nothing wrong with that.

If Jesus had returned to earth at the time when the Church of England (or the Episcopal Church of the USA) was debating the ordination of women to the priesthood, what would he have said about the debates? Which side would he have been on? What would he have thought of the personal views which opponents or supporters of the ordination of women took up? Of their motivations, of their characters? These may seem strange questions to ask. Nevertheless they can legitimately be asked, provided one is careful about how one uses the evidence of the New Testament to answer them. A few New Testament scholars would be prepared to ask such questions, in the belief that Christians should work through in their own minds what Jesus might have done or thought about a particular theological, or moral, or personal dilemma. It is as legitimate to ask questions of this sort of Jesus as it is to construct complex doctrines about him, such as the traditional doctrines of the Trinity or the incarnation.

Hence, unless Christians can know something about Jesus, and be sure that he is the sort of moral example they can truly follow, Christianity has very little on which to base its beliefs. A faith which is recognizably Christian — as opposed to merely believing in God or in the value of love — does require believing and knowing certain things about Jesus.

Was Jesus God?

The whole thrust of this chapter has been to suggest that for many Christians, this question will be of secondary importance to the question of whether Jesus revealed God in a way that is decisive for Christian moral beliefs and capable of inspiring Christian living — as most liberal theologians have thought. However, the question, 'Was Jesus God?' can still legitimately be asked, even given the doubts that must attach to the traditional doctrines which were developed in the early Church.

Knowing that the traditional doctrines may legitimately be questioned, modern theologians have tended to broaden the question, so that it is no longer put in terms of 'Was Jesus the second person of the Trinity incarnate?' A more modern way of putting it might be, 'Did Jesus have a unique experience of God which made him into the loving, self-sacrificial figure he was?' If so, was his experience due to God's special decision to make this particular man the means of redeeming the world? Or was Jesus' divine status the product of cultural or social evolutionary forces at work in the history of Israel, so that we can see his life as the culmination of human seeking for God, rather than God's seeking to redeem humankind?

Most theologians, of course, would answer that in Jesus God actively brought to fulfilment the plan for the salvation of human beings that he had prepared in the history of Israel, his chosen people. But that does not prevent the question being asked, and some theologians, who dislike the idea of God actively intervening in the world through miracles or through special divine action in the case of one human being, have preferred the evolutionary answer. But even these observations remain at the level of philosophical speculation about the nature of God's action in the world in general, rather than observation of Jesus' life; they still do not get to the point of the question, was Jesus God?

But there is one feature of Jesus' life which brings us back to the origins of belief in his divinity, and which, when its full importance is considered, clearly requires Christians to believe that Jesus was more than simply a teacher or a moral example, important though that is. This feature of Jesus' life is, of course, what happened after it had been completed — the resurrection, which makes Jesus the Lord of the Church and the Kingdom of God.

As an historical event, the nature of the resurrection is open to question and debate; the Gospel stories of Jesus' empty tomb and resurrection appearances to the disciples, for example, are as much attempts to explain or interpret the idea of resurrection as they are evidence for its occurrence; but the same cannot be said of the actual experience of Jesus as risen which the disciples had: this was the basis of early Christian thought and preaching about him, something behind which it does not seem possible for either speculative theology or biblical scholarship to penetrate. It is the experience of Jesus as risen Lord of the Church which gives continuity to Christian faith throughout the centuries, and it is this very real continuity of experience which provides the justificiation for believing that the traditional doctrines about Jesus still have an important place in theology, whatever may be the difficulties of the early Church's formulation of them, some of which we have looked at briefly in this chapter.

It is this experience which, above all speculative and historical arguments, justifies Christians today in holding to the belief that Jesus is God, and ensures that Christians at the beginning of Jesus' third millennium profess the same faith as was taught at the beginning of his first.

Epilogue

Jesus now and then — except that seems to be the one thing that you cannot do with him, to consider him 'now and then', to take him or to leave him, occasionally, on and off. In this book, we began by noticing that two thousand years later, people still seem to be obsessed with the person of Jesus of Nazareth, both Christians and non-Christians alike. Within the churches and at the box-office, Jesus continues to be a big hit. Yet, any historical reconstruction of him can only note that he spent his entire life in an obscure backwater of the Roman empire, never married, never wrote anything and was executed after a brief period of teaching and healing. What is it about this one man which has exercised such a fascination over two millennia?

In the first part of this book, we looked at what we can know about him and the impact he had on people of his own day, considering the resources available to a historian. While we can rediscover something of his ministry and the circumstances leading to his death, the crucial event is what happened to him afterwards. The books of the New Testament only came into being because of Jesus, and the conviction of the early Christians that God had raised him from the dead. Those early letters and Gospel accounts struggle to understand who Jesus was and is, and how God was so involved in his life and ministry, death and resurrection that they could see Jesus as God's agent fulfilling all the ancient Jewish hopes, that he had come from God, was with God — and even perhaps could be described as God himself.

The second half took the story on through the first few centuries with how the early Christians handled the teaching of Jesus and the central role he came to play in their worship. However, it was the attempt to answer the questions about Jesus' identity and his relationship to God both philosophically and theologically which led to the great councils of the Church and the classic formulations of the creeds and definitions of the Trinity and the incarnation — that God is Three in One, and that Jesus is both divine and human. Finally, we have brought the story back up to date with the attempts to re-express those beliefs within modern and even postmodern culture, leading to a range of contemporary views from liberals and conservatives alike, within and outside the churches.

Common to it all has emerged the conviction that, whatever else happens, we cannot leave Jesus alone — or is that Jesus cannot leave us alone? There has to be some connection between 'then' and 'now', between the historical Jesus and our reconstructions about him, between those early beliefs in forming the Christian tradition and the churches today. To make those connections, giving it attention occasionally 'now and then' will never be enough. Over two thousand years of history confront us today, and the events 'then' impact on us 'now': who is Jesus of Nazareth? What do we make of him? And what does he make of us?

References and Further Reading

Chapter 1: Jesus Now and Then

W. Barnes Tatum, *Jesus at the Movies: A Guide to the First Hundred Years* (Santa Rosa, Calif.: Polebridge Press, 1997). An interesting discussion of Hollywood's fascination with Jesus.

PART I: THE NEW TESTAMENT

While these books are listed according to the chapter to which they best relate, most of them deal with many of the issues raised throughout Part I.

Chapter 2: The Historical Jesus

Graham N. Stanton, *The Gospels and Jesus*, 2nd ed. (Oxford University Press, 2002). The second part is a well-written and clear introduction to the life and ministry of Jesus.

E. P. Sanders, *The Historical Figure of Jesus* (Harmondsworth: Penguin, 1993). A readable account of Jesus from a leading New Testament scholar whose work has re-emphasized Jesus' Jewish setting.

Gerd Theissen and Annette Merz, *The Historical Jesus: A Comprehensive Guide* (London: SCM Press, 1998). A long and detailed workbook for the sources and accounts of Jesus' activity.

N. T. Wright, *Jesus and the Victory of God* (London: SPCK, 1996). A good introduction to the historical quests and the modern debate between the 'Californian school' and the 'Third Questers', followed by Tom Wright's own detailed reconstruction of Jesus.

Chapter 3: Jesus in the Gospels

Graham N. Stanton, *The Gospels and Jesus*, 2nd ed. (Oxford University Press, 2002). The first part considers each of the Gospels in turn.

Richard A. Burridge, *Four Gospels, One Jesus?* (London: SPCK and Grand Rapids: Eerdmans, 1994). A symbolic reading of the four portraits in the Gospels and a discussion of unity and diversity.

Richard A. Burridge, *What Are the Gospels? A Comparison with Graeco-Roman Biography* (Cambridge University Press, 1992; updated edition, Grand Rapids: Eerdmans, 2004). My revision of my doctoral thesis on the genre of the Gospels.

Chapter 4: Jesus and Paul

E. P. Sanders, *Paul*, Past Master Series (Oxford University Press, 1991). A short, clear and readable introduction from the scholar whose reinterpretation of Paul and Palestinian Judaism has overturned many Protestant or Lutheran readings of Paul.

J. D. G. Dunn, *The Theology of Paul the Apostle* (Edinburgh: T&T Clark and Grand Rapids: Eerdmans, 1998). A large and comprehensive treatment.

Chapter 5: New Testament Views of Jesus

Ben Witherington III, *The Many Faces of the Christ: The Christologies of the New Testament and Beyond* (New York: Crossroad, 1998). An accessible account of the different pictures of Jesus in the Gospels, Paul and the rest of the New Testament which argues for a variety of understandings.

Christopher Tuckett, *Christology and the New Testament: Jesus and His Earliest Followers* (Louisville: Westminster John Knox, 2001). A very useful text-book, covering the whole of the New Testament, raising questions about Jesus' own self-understanding and its relevance for today.

PART II: THE EARLY CHURCH

Many of the quotations from the early Christian writers in Part II are taken from, or based on, the translations in J. Stevenson (revised by W. H. C. Frend), *A New Eusebius*, 2nd ed. (London: SPCK, 1987) and *Creeds, Councils and Controversies*, 2nd ed. (London: SPCK, 1989). These are the most useful collections of sources for early Christianity. Also quoted are H. Bettenson, *The Early Christian Fathers* (Oxford University Press, 1956) and *The Later Christian Fathers* (Oxford University Press, 1970).

A good introduction to the early Church is S. G. Hall, *Doctrine and Practice in the Early Church* (London: SPCK, 1991).

Much fuller accounts are to be found in:

H. Chadwick, *The Church in Ancient Society. From Galilee to Gregory the Great* (Oxford University Press, 2001).

W. H. C. Frend, *The Rise of Christianity* (London: Darton, Longman & Todd, 1984).

Chapter 6: The Early Church and the Teaching of Jesus

The translations of Justin *(First Apology)* and Origen *(Against Celsus)* used in this chapter are:

St Justin Martyr. The First and Second Apologies, translated by L. W. Barnard (Ancient Christian Writers, 56; New York/Mahwah, N.J.: Paulist Press, 1997).

Origen Contra Celsum, translated by Henry Chadwick (Cambridge University Press, 1953).

Extracts from 2 *Clement* are taken from *The Apostolic Fathers*, translated by J. B. Lightfoot and J. R. Harmer, revised by Michael W. Holmes (Leicester: Apollos, 1989), pp. 68-78.

Other translations of Ignatius of Antioch, Justin, and 2 *Clement* may be found in *Early Christian Fathers*, translated by Cyril C. Richardson et al. (The Library of Christian Classics, 1; London: SCM Press, 1953) and of Ignatius and the *Letter to Diognetus* in M. Staniforth (revised by A. Louth), *Early Christian Writings*, 2nd ed. (Harmondsworth: Penguin Classics, 1987).

H. Chadwick, *Early Christian Thought and the Classical Tradition* (Oxford University Press, 1966). A very good set of essays on Justin, Clement of Alexandria, and Origen.

R. M. Grant, *Greek Apologists of the Second Century* (London: SCM Press, 1988). A clear concise account of Christian apologetic.

R. Stark, *The Rise of Christianity. A Sociologist Reconsiders History* (Princeton University Press, 1996). A provocative (and not always convincing) attempt to interpret Christianity as a middle-class religion fully at home in Greco-Roman society.

Chapter 7: Jesus in Early Christian Worship

An invaluable collection of early prayers associated with the Eucharist is R. C. D. Jasper and G. J. Cuming, *Prayers of the Eucharist: Early and Reformed,* 3rd ed. (New York: Pueblo, 1987).

Complete translations of the *Didache* may be found in the volumes edited by Richardson and Staniforth mentioned above. The most recent translation of the *Apostolic Tradition* is Alistair Stewart-Sykes, *Hippolytus. On the Apostolic Tradition* (New York: St Vladimir's Seminary Press, 2001).

P. F. Bradshaw, *Early Christian Worship: A Basic Introduction to Ideas and Practice* (London: SPCK, 1996). A short and accessible work by a leading liturgical scholar.

E. C. Whitaker, *Documents of the Baptismal Liturgy* (London: SPCK, 1970). Texts in translation.

Chapter 8: Jesus — Divine and Human

R. M. Grant, *Jesus after the Gospels: The Christ of the Second Century* (London: SCM Press, 1990). A straightforward introduction to some of the ideas and writers.

J. N. D. Kelly, *Early Christian Doctrines,* 5th ed. (London: A. & C. Black, 1977). Still the best history of early Christian doctrine.

N. Russell, *Cyril of Alexandria* (London: Longmans, 2000). Contains a good account of the controversy over the person of Christ in the fifth century.

M. F. Wiles, *Archetypal Heresy: Arianism through the Centuries* (Oxford University Press, 1996). Covers not only the early Church but the arguments of eighteenth-century anti-Trinitarians such as William Whiston.

F. M. Young, *The Making of the Creeds* (London: SCM Press, 1991).

Chapter 9: Modern Understandings of Jesus

C. Gunton, *Yesterday and Today: A Study of Continuities in Christology*, 2nd ed. (London: SPCK, 1997). An important study by a leading conservative theologian.

B. L. Hebblethwaite, *The Incarnation: Collected Essays in Christology* (Cambridge University Press, 1987). Fairly untechnical essays, cautiously defending the traditional doctrines.

J. Hick (ed.), *The Myth of God Incarnate* (London: SCM Press, 1977). Most famous statement of the case for a liberal reinterpretation of traditional Christology.

J. L. Houlden, *Jesus: A Question of Identity* (London: SPCK, 1992). A liberal view of Jesus based on sound New Testament and historical scholarship.

R. Swinburne, *The Christian God* (Oxford University Press, 1995) and *The Resurrection of God Incarnate* (Oxford University Press, 2003). Defence of traditional Christian beliefs from a philosophical perspective: Enlightenment method but conservative conclusions.

M. F. Wiles, *A Shared Search* (London: SCM Press, 1994), chapters 12 and 13. Brief considerations of how to use the figure of Jesus in Christian theology today.

R. D. Williams, *Resurrection. Interpreting the Easter Gospel* (London: Darton, Longman & Todd, 1982). An important example of the work of a leading theologian who transcends the liberal/conservative divide.